Voices of the Voiceless

Voices of the Voiceless

Religion, Communism, and the Keston Archive

JULIE deGRAFFENRIED
ZOE KNOX

editors

1845BOOKS

TO THE VOICELESS

Contents

List of Essays

Foreword

MICHAEL BOURDEAUX

Sir John Lawrence, the first president of Keston College, dated religious *samizdat* to a scrap of paper he discovered under the pillow in his hotel room soon after the restoration of his visa following the death of Stalin in 1953. "Help us believers!" was the essence of the message. Long before my commission in 1965—"Be our voice" was the urgent message of a group of Ukrainian women, members of the Orthodox Church—I had begun collecting information on the persecution of religion in general. I simply bought it from a kiosk on a Moscow street.

Science and Religion (*Nauka i religiia*) began publication in September 1959, the month of my arrival in the Soviet Union as a member of the first-ever British exchange group to spend an academic year there. Consequently, my initial purchase inaugurated the complete series held in the Keston Archive. The magazine became the banner of the renewed persecution initiated by Nikita Khrushchev.

The Russian Orthodox Church attracted both John and me, but the written word compelled us to the defense of religion and of spiritual values as a whole. It was these that *Nauka i religiia* indiscriminately attacked. It is these that form the broadest possible spectrum of the holdings in the Keston Archive at Baylor University. It is these that, in microcosm, the present volume reflects. In its variety it is like a medieval squint into the richness of the body of the church, allowing a glimpse of its breadth and complexity.

From its modest origins the collection began to grow, almost imperceptibly at first, but then at times with a deluge of new material. I supplemented my reading of the monthly issues of the atheist magazine by scanning the Soviet press, cutting and pasting articles under various headings—Orthodox, Baptist, Catholic, Jewish, Muslim, and Buddhist—so the outline of a system began to take shape.

The Khrushchev regime's new wave of repression stimulated a spate of new religious writing, circulated in samizdat. Paradoxically, persecution led directly to an enormous increase in written support for Christianity and its values, as the Keston collection generously attests.

Samizdat did not, however, originate in the 1960s. Thirty years earlier a group of Orthodox bishops, imprisoned in the remote Arctic island fastness of Solovki, appealed for justice in a letter smuggled to Moscow. Book-length spiritual testimonies circulated in the 1930s, several of which are in the holdings and one of which is described in this volume.

However, it was the Baptists who seized the initiative in the early 1960s. The persecuted *Initsiativniki* (who took the *initiative* in demanding a congress to formulate a defense of their rights) somehow coordinated their efforts and established "export" channels to communicate their cause worldwide in a way no other religious group achieved at the time. The writings of Orthodox believers dating from the 1960s and continuing to the 1980s were richer and more varied in content, but they never coalesced into a movement.

From the beginning, scattered information on Judaism, Islam, and Buddhism filtered its way into the archive, but it was with the expansion of the staff in the 1970s that the deposited materials began to take on a richer aspect: Catholic documents from Lithuania and Ukraine began to show as much coordination as that of the Baptists. Keston now had specialists who could translate and codify information in languages other than Russian (over twenty at its height).

The gradual easing of stringent measures—or sometimes the threat of their increase—led to believers in many other countries of the Soviet bloc finding their voice: Poles, Hungarians, Romanians, East Germans, and Czechs are all reflected in this volume.

One article notes with regret that the drying up of funding prevented continuation of the research at a particularly interesting time in the 1990s, but at least the work continues with ongoing improvements for the archive at Baylor University, the acquisition of new materials, and the publication—in Russian—of an encyclopedia on religion in Russia today.

Foreword

KATHY R. HILLMAN

Stories chronicling courage in the face of religious persecution, antireligious materials, government publications, *samizdat*, personal papers, and other items fill the third floor of the F. L. Carroll Library in the heart of the Baylor University campus in Waco, Texas. A Baptist school in the United States hardly seems a likely location for archived reports of spiritual oppression half a world away. Yet, when Keston College in Oxford in the United Kingdom sought a repository for their comprehensive library and archives on religious persecution under communist and other totalitarian regimes, Baylor answered the call.

In what many might have viewed as an unlikely marriage, then Baylor's Dean of the College of Arts & Sciences and Soviet scholar Wallace Daniel saw a potential match. In 1957, Baylor had established the J.M. Dawson Institute of Church-State Studies dedicated to religious liberty and research in religion, politics, and society. Fortunately, Keston trustees agreed that the two institutes—Keston and Dawson—shared common concerns, common visions, and common commitments. On June 21, 2007, Keston College and Baylor University signed a contract transferring the Keston Collection to Baylor while the university agreed to create a research facility known as the Michael Bourdeaux Research Center and to establish the Keston Center for Religion, Politics, and Society as part of the J.M. Dawson Institute.

Later that year, the precious materials, carefully collected by Keston and categorized by country and religious group, arrived in Waco. The hundreds of shipping boxes contained Keston News Service press clippings, pamphlets, reports, manuscripts, court documents, and bibliographies as well as 4,500 photographs, 17 works of art, 738 audiovisual items, 69 propaganda posters, rare artifacts, and more. A library of about 8,000 books and nearly 900 periodicals and serials accompanied the 1,400 linear feet of archives created in at least 33 languages and encompassing 30 discreet denominations and religions. The scope included not only the former Soviet Union and other Warsaw Pact countries but also nations as diverse as Angola, Afghanistan, Cuba, China, Vietnam, and Mozambique. Organizing, processing, and hosting researchers soon began.

The narrative continued in 2012 when the Keston Center became a part of the Baylor University Libraries. The Michael Bourdeaux Research Center still beckons Baylor students and faculty as well as scholars from around the world to explore stories not yet told, to discover images still filed away, to uncover letters long forgotten, and to piece together the scattered truths of individuals, families, churches, communities, denominations, and religions across countries and time. Today, the Keston Center hosts lectures, symposia, panels, and commemorations to highlight the collection and bear witness to those who defended religious freedom, often at great personal cost.

The story doesn't end, and the stories don't end. The pages of this volume testify to that, and additional ones await the telling as Baylor's Keston Center continues Michael Bourdeaux's and Keston College's call to be "the voice of the voiceless" yesterday, today, and tomorrow.

Acknowledgments

We have received support from many quarters during our work on this book. We appreciate the staff at Baylor University Libraries' commitment to the project, among them John Wilson, Interim Dean of University Libraries; Kathy Hillman, Director of the Keston Center for Religion, Politics, and Society; and Carlye Thornton, Communications Coordinator and Digital Design Specialist. Larisa Seago, the Keston collection's archivist, has been tireless in her work and always ready and willing to respond to our many and varied questions. Likewise, we thank Carey Newman, Savanah Landerholm, Jenny Hunt, and the scrupulous staff at Baylor University Press for "adopting" this book and bringing it to fruition.

We are extremely grateful to Keston Institute UK, whose support made possible a very productive and stimulating week of working together in the Keston Archive. Our collaboration on this book would not have been possible without twenty-first century technologies—we've exchanged hundreds of emails over the past eighteen months, shared images and draft documents through cloud computing, and spent dozens of hours in virtual meetings—but that single week together was critical for formulating our ideas on how best to showcase the archive's many treasures.

Stella Rock and Wallace Daniel offered us valuable feedback on a draft of the introduction. Adina Kelley provided much-needed assistance with details great and small. We are grateful to our families for their support and especially for their patience with our many late-night and holiday-season Skype sessions.

Above all, we would like to thank the sixteen individuals who selected images and wrote essays for this book. When we invited them to contribute, we had no idea what they might pick. Imagine our fascination and delight when they chose photographs, petitions, paintings, underground literature, bedsheets, and more besides. Every contributor has taught us something new and encouraged us either to look afresh at familiar topics or to discover new ones. That these images and essays are the tip of the iceberg might be seen as either overwhelming or inspiring, but either way it begs further work in this invaluable archive.

Every effort has been made to trace the copyright holders for the artwork and imagery included in this book. Readers can contact Baylor University Press directly if they believe that they are the rightful owner of any of the images reproduced here, so we can acknowledge copyright as appropriate in any future editions.

Julie deGraffenried
Waco, USA

Zoe Knox
Leicester, UK

Introduction

New Voices

Activists, Archivists, and Academics on the Keston Collection

JULIE deGRAFFENRIED AND ZOE KNOX

The October Revolution of 1917 brought radical change to the former Russian Empire. The Bolsheviks came to power with an agenda that sought nothing less than the complete transformation of politics, economics, society, and culture. The revolutionary regime passed legislation mandating the separation of church and state as early as January 1918, a move accompanied by anticlerical and, soon, atheist propaganda. Bolshevik authorities had little interest in preserving the power or influence of Russian Orthodoxy, Russia's traditional faith, which they viewed as a leftover from the backward, patriarchal past used by the privileged elite to oppress the peasantry and the workers. New laws that severely restricted religious practice, massive church closures, and arrests of clergy in the late 1920s and 1930s created an assault on religion unprecedented in history. Initially targeting the Russian Orthodox Church (ROC), the state antireligious campaign soon expanded to include all of the Soviet Union's hundreds of faiths. The goal of communist religious policy appeared to be the eradication of religion.

A brief respite from the persecution of religion occurred during World War II when faith suddenly intersected with support for the war effort and foreign policy concerns. In 1943, appealing to nationalist sentiments, Joseph Stalin allowed the ROC to elect a patriarch and to open a theological institute in Moscow. During and immediately after the war, the Soviet Union expanded its territory to include the Baltics and parts of eastern Europe. New mechanisms for controlling rather than simply eliminating religious communities via state agencies emerged, such as the Council for the Affairs of the Orthodox Church and the Council for the Affairs of Religious Cults. The expansion of the Kremlin's influence across eastern Europe following World War II imposed Soviet religious policy across what became known as the Soviet bloc. A renewed assault on faith communities in the form of more church closures, vigorous atheist propaganda and education, and severe restrictions on proselytization occurred in the Khrushchev era, becoming particularly active after 1959. Official religious organizations and state authorities paid lip service to the constitutionally enshrined right to freedom of religion while foreign observers were duly trotted to working places of worship and interviews with approved spokespersons.[1]

Seeking to counter the official Soviet line on religion by revealing the reality "on the ground" for believers, Rev. Canon Dr. Michael Bourdeaux and Sir John Lawrence founded the Centre for the Study of Religion and Communism—later renamed Keston College—in 1969, as recounted in Xenia Dennen's essay in this book. The organization focused mainly on the Soviet Union and Soviet bloc but also collected information on other leftist regimes such as in Afghanistan, China, Cuba, and Vietnam. Keston College served as a clearinghouse of sorts, receiving and processing information to distribute to policy makers, rights groups, and news agencies. Although chartered as an educational charity, and ostensibly neutral, the passion of Keston's personnel and the uses of its information required a delicate dance along the line between impartiality and activism. In the global political context of the Cold War, Keston's material became a weapon in the hands of the West. As Alyona Kojevnikov recalls, in their heyday, both Keston College and its periodical *Keston News Service* were an integral part of global networks related to human rights activism and reporting, legal battles brought by dissidents inspired by the Helsinki Accords after the mid-1970s, and politicking by cold warriors such as British Prime Minister Margaret Thatcher and United States President Ronald Reagan in the 1980s.

---

1   For more detailed discussion, see Zoe Knox, "Russian Religious Life in the Soviet Era," in *The Oxford Handbook of Russian Religious Thought*, ed. Randall Poole, George Patterson, and Caryl Emerson (Oxford: Oxford University Press, forthcoming).

The Soviet religious landscape began to change in the late 1980s when Mikhail Gorbachev's radical reforms eventually led to an end to antireligious propaganda, state-sanctioned religious persecution, and severe legal restrictions on religious groups. The thousand-year anniversary of the introduction of Christianity to Kievan Rus' in 988 gave the Orthodox Church a new level of visibility and, thus, legitimacy. This new freedom soon extended to other faiths and spread to eastern Europe: communist parties throughout the Soviet bloc followed the Kremlin's lead and demonstrated an unprecedented tolerance toward faith communities and their activities. Michael Long captures the energy and ambitions of unofficial church groups in East Germany at the time

Michael Bourdeaux and Russian Baptist dissident Georgi Vins, 1979.

in his examination of an issue of *Forum for Church and Human Rights*, an Evangelical Lutheran newsletter. He also highlights the intimate connection of churches with dissident movements. The collapse of communist regimes throughout eastern Europe in 1989 and the dissolution of the USSR in 1991 triggered a reinvigoration of religious life. Traditional churches in particular enjoyed a resurgence as they became a core constituent of post-communist national identities.

Although its original mission to record abuses against believers behind the Iron Curtain rather abruptly concluded, Keston Institute UK continues to be very active as an educational charity, supporting original research into religion under communist regimes and sponsoring the massive encyclopedia project, a multivolume survey of contemporary religious life across all of Russia.[2] Roman Lunkin discusses photographs of Buddhist and Shamanic structures taken during a project field trip to Siberia in 2009. Keston also continues to play a vital role in uncovering the history of religion and belief throughout the Soviet bloc. The materials collected from its foundation in 1969 until monitoring operations

2   See, for example, Kestonskii institut, *Religiozno-obshchestvennaia zhizn' rossiiskikh regionov*, Tom 1 (Moscow: Letnii Sad, 2014).

Keston College archivist Malcolm Walker, date uncertain.

ceased in the mid-1990s are preserved in the Keston Archive and Library, which is housed in its entirety in the Keston Center for Religion, Politics, and Society, at Baylor University in Waco, Texas. The collection is accessible to any serious researcher.

We have asked a number of people connected to the Keston Archive to select an item from the collection they found particularly stimulating, significant, or surprising and to write about it. Many of the contributors are scholars who have worked with Keston's archival materials in the course of their own research over the past decade. Others are former or current Keston personnel from both sides of the Atlantic. Some are clergy; some are heavily involved in human rights activism. They come from different parts of the world and different generations. As much as possible, we have tried to allow their voices to speak freely, to reflect each contributor's unique perspective on the material he or she has accessed.

Although the items highlighted here are not representative of the Keston Archive's contents as a whole, they are entirely representative of the types and range of materials with which researchers have worked in the past and that future researchers might expect to find in the collection. A large percentage of the archival holdings, as one might expect, are textual documents, but here the reader will find not only texts but also photographs, posters, petitions, and paintings. The latter tend to be visually striking; the former not so much—and for good reason.

The creators of underground literature, letters, reports, and newsletters meant them to be inconspicuous in order to avoid detection. Behind any "uninteresting" typescript document, consider the homemade printing press, illegally used typewriter, and human chain of smugglers needed to generate and circulate it. While a significant portion of the archive's holdings focus on Russia and Russian Orthodoxy, the contributors' choices vary in place, faith community, and genre.

A number of common themes unite this seemingly disparate collection of items. The first of these is the ongoing practice of religion by ordinary citizens despite the sustained efforts of communist authorities to suppress it. Scholars call the everyday expressions of faith by believers "lived religion," or sometimes "vernacular religion," a concept particularly used by ethnographers to obtain a more holistic understanding of religious life than can be gained by studying religious institutions or formalized rites and rituals alone. Lived religion is an especially fruitful phenomenon to examine in contexts in which religious institutions are constrained by the state, as was the case in the Soviet bloc, when individuals and communities might express faith entirely independently of the oversight (or even sanction) of religious authorities. Accounts issued by church dignitaries or reports compiled by the state do not reliably indicate how believers experienced or enacted their faith on an everyday level. A prime example is pilgrimage. In the USSR, the Soviet authorities banned some Orthodox pilgrimages with the support of church officials. In spite of this, pilgrims continued the practice without official sanction or any clerical involvement.[3] They also continued to frequent the few functioning Orthodox monasteries as Stella Rock's examination of a photograph of pilgrims at a monastery in Pskov in Soviet Russia reveals. Like many items in the Keston Archive, it is unclear how the photograph entered the collection: the risk associated with documenting aspects of religious life and especially conveying information to the West means that the provenance of much of the material is obscure.[4] Rock's commentary shows that, in this case at least, pilgrimage thrived despite the authorities' restrictions. (It also illustrates that archival research often poses as many questions as it answers.) Sonja Luehrmann discusses notes left on the fence surrounding St. Ksenia's chapel in Leningrad (since renamed St. Petersburg) and shines a light on the way some

3   See Stella Rock, "'They Burned the Pine, but the Place Remains All the Same': Pilgrimage in the Changing Landscape of Soviet Russia," in *State Secularism and Lived Religion in Soviet Russia and Ukraine*, ed. Catherine Wanner (Oxford: Oxford University Press, 2012), 159–89.

4   See the discussion in Sonja Luehrmann, *Religion in Secular Archives: Soviet Atheism and Historical Knowledge* (Oxford: Oxford University Press, 2015), 153.

Orthodox believers related to this saint. These two contributions illustrate how ordinary believers continued to practice their faith both in dialogue with and beyond the purview of the institutional churches. Moreover, without the approval of communist authorities, activities like participating in a pilgrimage or leaving prayers for saints might be framed as acts of dissent; communism's ideological monopoly meant that even religious belief mounted a challenge to the state.

Front page of French human rights newspaper
Catacombes, October 15, 1971.

Several contributors to this book highlight the activities of religious communities confined to the underground. The communist authorities regarded some faiths as more dangerous than others and sought to fully eradicate them. True Orthodox Christians, who belonged to a Russian Orthodox schism, refused to acknowledge the authority of either church or state and operated entirely clandestinely. Tatiana Spektor (Nun Alexandra) shares her conclusion following research into the case of Raisa Ivanova, a True Orthodox woman who died in a special psychiatric prison in Kazan in Soviet Russia. Although the underground bulletin that she examines was more circumspect, Spektor states that prison officials murdered Ivanova for her intransigence. The Soviet government required Pentecostals to register with the state not as an identifiable community but as part of the All-Union Council of Evangelical Christians-Baptists, an administrative body that accepted the state's strictures on religious life. The effort to remove any trace of Pentecostals from the religious landscape led many of them to reject the legal obligation to register and to continue their practices underground. Emily B. Baran discusses the "Siberian Seven," surely one of the most intriguing episodes in the history of religion and the Cold War. Frustrated by the refusal of Soviet officials to grant them the right to emigrate, seven members of two Pentecostal families from Siberia sought refuge in the American Embassy in Moscow, living in the basement for four years. Baran has selected a photograph taken as one of the women was transferred from the embassy to the hospital following a hunger strike.

A third theme in this collection is the profound challenge posed to the atheist and antireligious campaign by underground literature, or *samizdat*. The word samizdat derives from the Russian *sam* ("self" or "by oneself") and *izdat* (short for publishing house), usually translated in English as "self-published." The Keston Archive includes more than 4,000 such items, making it the largest collection of religion-related samizdat in the world.[5] This literature was produced and circulated without official approval and thus evaded the censors. Religious samizdat took a wide variety of forms. The bulletin produced by the Council of Prisoners' Relatives in the USSR, discussed by April L. French, subverted the attempts of communist authorities to control information regarding the incarceration of believers, in this case Baptists and Evangelical Christians. As French explains, the women behind the bulletin sought to publicize the plight of prisoners of conscience to international audiences. Closely related to samizdat was *tamizdat*, from the Russian word *tam* ("there") and usually translated as "published there," underground literature smuggled out of the communist bloc and published in the West, often in translation. Wallace L. Daniel discusses Aleksandr Men's book *Son of Man*. A Russian Orthodox priest and theologian, Men preached an open, tolerant, and ecumenical version of Orthodoxy and emphasized hands-on pastoral work. He drew a large number of intellectuals to Orthodoxy, which authorities found unpalatable, and hence much of his prolific writing circulated only

---

5   Kathy Hillman and Larisa Seago, "Alive and Available," *Christian Librarian* 64 (2014): 40.

despre
IUBIRE

despre
MUNCĂ

clandestinely. The production of these publications, not to mention the smuggling of them to the West, carried great risk for those involved. Long presents a miniature version of Zdeněk Mlynář's memoir, a tamizdat publication designed for smuggling into Czechoslovakia and an example of the kind of "crossover" human rights material available among Keston's religion-focused holdings.

The state's persecution of religious communities and individual believers runs like a red thread through the diverse group of items presented in this collection. In some cases, persecution was via legal means, as shown by Michael Bourdeaux's discussion of the trial of Aida Skripnikova, a young Baptist woman from Leningrad. After a sympathizer smuggled the transcript of her trial out of the USSR, Skripnikova's conviction in 1968 gained the attention of the international community. The transcript was handwritten onto twenty-two strips of a bedsheet, a striking and moving artifact attesting to the state's use of the legal system as a tool to silence the faithful.[6] Authorities made calculated efforts to muz-

---

6 Keston's revelations of Skripnikova's treatment galvanized British Christians into action, prompting a letter-writing campaign that lobbied British foreign office officials to raise her case, and that of religious persecution more broadly, with

Romanian drawings, likely from Romanian Orthodox group Lord's Army and likely for children: "About Love," "About Work," "About Steadfastness." Date uncertain.

zle and intimidate religious communities, as shown in the image from Hungary selected by Julie deGraffenried. The photograph shows a stakeout of a Methodist congregation in Hungary, a striking reminder that communist states' expansive surveillance apparatuses monitored not only religious dignitaries but also ordinary congregants. To marginalize religion, states used incarceration in prisons, labor camps, and psychiatric hospitals. Keston's work in publicizing the cases of individual prisoners of conscience—in some instances leading to release—is revealed in the case of Dorel Cataramă, a Romanian Adventist, as Alina Urs explains in her essay.[7] The extensive evidence Keston collected to produce prisoner

their Soviet counterparts. See "Aida and the British Public," *Protestant Communities in the USSR*, accessed July 19, 2018, https://www.dhi.ac.uk/protestantizm/section/?section=aida.

7   See, for example, these publications that included profiles of individual prisoners of conscience, providing details of their religious affiliation, alleged crimes, sentences, and even the addresses of their family members: Keston College, *Religious Prisoners in the USSR* (Keston, UK: Greenfire Books, 1987) and Amnesty International, *Prisoners of Conscience in the USSR: Their Treatment and Conditions* (London: A. I. Publications, 1975).

profiles has led one researcher to liken this archival material to police files on criminal suspects.[8]

The illicit networks that connected religious dissidents both with each other and with western sympathizers is another theme that emerges from this collection of images and essays. Samizdat circulated through expansive underground networks that sought to disseminate information about state campaigns within and between faith communities and to human rights activists and coreligionists abroad. Tat'iana Goricheva's statement of support for a fellow dissident highlights the close links between dissident communities in the USSR, maintained and fostered because of (and despite) the oppressive environment for believers. As Elizabeth Skomp notes, the statement not only circulated in samizdat but appeared in *Russian Thought (Russkaia Mysl')*, a Russian-language newspaper published in France, thus pointing to the important role of the Russian émigré community in publicizing rights abuses in its homeland. Dissident networks provided Keston College with the raw material on which to base its assessment of religious life in the communist bloc. Mark Hurst presents an internal document detailing the procedure for processing incoming material and passing new information on to "targets" through press releases, news bulletins, books, and a journal. Keston fed information to human rights organizations like Amnesty International, western media outlets like Radio Free Europe/Radio Liberty, and Keston support groups abroad. The organization did not actively seek samizdat but instead became the destination for accounts of religious persecution by virtue of its expansive networks and profile in the region.[9]

Many of the photographs, documents, and artifacts in this book point to the central role of women of all ages in maintaining faith communities. Luehrmann identifies female authorship of many of the notes left at St. Ksenia's chapel, and Rock makes interesting observations about the presence of women at the Pskov pilgrimage. In these parlous conditions, many women stood firm in their faith, as observed in the account of Skripnikova's trial discussed by Bourdeaux and the case of Goricheva recounted by Skomp. Women were central in dissident circles, as evident in the bulletin of the Council of Prisoners' Relatives discussed by French. On the other side of the coin, communist governments highlighted the central role of women in maintaining religious practices within the family, albeit unwittingly.

---

8   Luehrmann, *Religion in Secular Archives*, 145.
9   Mark Hurst, *British Human Rights Organizations and Soviet Dissent, 1965–1985* (London: Bloomsbury, 2016), 123.

Even in the final decades of Soviet-style communism, official antireligious propaganda presented the archetypal believer as an aged female crone in order to cast the faithful as anachronistic and backward and a pernicious influence on children. One of the posters analyzed by deGraffenried stands out precisely because of its atypicality as it lampoons a male elderly figure rather than the usual female figure.

A final theme is the frustration of communist authorities with their progress in suppressing religion. Believers produced many of the items selected by contributors, thus evidencing the abject failure of atheist and antireligious campaigns across the communist bloc. This failure is also implicitly recognized in the material produced by state authorities. They provide evidence of the significant resources that the regimes poured into countering the influence of faith. The doggerel on one of the anti-Jehovah's Witnesses posters discussed by Zoe Knox indicates a desperation in the Soviet state's efforts to counter the growth of this religious group. The images of believers in antireligious propaganda point to the failure of the communist authorities to reach into the domestic realm. It was within the home that religious beliefs and practices were most often discussed, enacted, and ultimately transmitted to children. The inability of the state to successfully harness the family unit as a means of eliminating belief was a major obstacle to the campaign against religion. Instead, the family served as the locus of the reproduction of faith.[10]

We freely acknowledge the limitations of this collection of images and essays. The Keston Archive contains thousands of fascinating objects, any one of which might have been presented here. For example, the archive has a rare Buryat-language edition of the New Testament, recently produced for this

Cover from Soviet antireligious journal *Nauka i religiia*, February 2, 1960.

---

10 This is explored in Julie deGraffenried, "Combating God and Grandma: The Soviet Antireligious Campaigns and the Battle for Childhood," in *The Dangerous God: Christianity and the Soviet Experiment*, ed. Dominic Erdozain (DeKalb: Northern Illinois University Press, 2017), 32–50.

indigenous Siberian group; the candid memoir of Rev. Sydney Linton, chaplain at the British embassy in Moscow from 1948 to 1951; and some delightful drawings by members of Romanian Orthodox group the Lord's Army, most likely used for the religious instruction of children. Periodicals from the Soviet Union, such as *Nauka i religiia*, émigré journals, such as *Posev*, and human rights press, such as *Catacombes*, line the shelves of the reading room. At the time of writing, the archive's audio and video material has yet to be processed. Its untapped gems include an audio recording of Fr. Jerzy Popiełuszko, the Polish Roman Catholic priest, conducting a mass in Warsaw in 1983, the year before his brutal murder at the hands of the security police, and several recordings of Valery Barinov's Christian rock opera "Trumpet Call," recorded in Leningrad in the early 1980s. Some of the collection has yet to be declassified, and other items have been added or processed since the writing of this introduction. Some limits are imposed by the subjects or faith communities themselves, and at the most basic level, the project is limited by human memory (in the case of Keston personnel) and by the choice of topics and access (in the case of scholars).

No archival collection, however painstakingly curated, can ever fully represent the vitality, breadth, or depth of the religious experience. And yet, as these essays and images demonstrate, the remarkable resources contained in the Keston Archive provide a way to recapture and revive glimpses of the past. This unique collection is borne of a very different approach to its central subject than archives organized around official categories or focusing on state-produced material that largely inform historical analysis of religion in the region.[11] It offers a vast body of material on religion as it was lived under communist regimes, and on religious dissent across the Soviet bloc, as well as a window into how faith survived among the faithless.

---

11 Luehrmann calls it a "counter-archive" in Luehrmann, *Religion in Secular Archives*, 134–61.

1

Construction Fence Prayers in Leningrad

SONJA LUEHRMANN

"Blessed Ksenia, make Sasha fall in love with me and marry me." This prayer is one of dozens of handwritten pleas on a sign that barred entry to one of Leningrad's sacred places, the chapel erected over the presumed grave of Ksenia in the Smolensk Cemetery. "The chapel building is in a state of collapse. Entry strictly forbidden," reads the printed text. Churches, mosques, synagogues, and temples that were hazardous to enter were a common sight in the Soviet Union—often as a result of deliberate neglect on the part of government agencies that had little interest in making them accessible.

In the case of Ksenia's chapel, the construction fence separated believers from a much-loved intercessor: Ksenia Petrova (ca. 1730–1803), a resident of St. Petersburg who experienced early widowhood after her husband, an army officer and liturgical chanter, died of a sudden illness. She became a fool for Christ's sake, an Orthodox Christian trickster figure who voluntarily renounces sanity and social standing but is often considered to have prophetic gifts. Ksenia lived on the streets, asked people to call her by her late husband's name, and helped build the Smolensk Cemetery church by secretly bringing bricks at night. After her death, she was buried in the cemetery. Although she was not officially canonized until 1988, the chapel erected over her gravesite in 1902 is a testament to her widespread veneration in imperial Russia.

A series of photos from 1984 to 1985 show that this popular devotion was alive and well by the end of the Soviet period. Closed since 1962, the chapel had

recently been returned to the Russian Orthodox Church and was being restored in time for the celebrations of the millennium of Christianity in Russia. As an urban laywoman, Ksenia was closer to modern city dwellers than many other Russian Orthodox saints and was known to lend an understanding ear to everyday concerns. The prayers written on the sign and etched into the wooden fence read like a catalogue of worries of the average Soviet citizen. "Blessed Ksenia, help me find a place to live." "b.K., give health to my son."

In addition to students asking for success in exams, marriage and kinship are major themes in the prayers. Often reported from a female perspective, some tell family dramas in a nutshell. "Blessed Ksenia, help me in the struggle with the relatives of my husband, let me keep the dacha, don't let them rob me." "Blessed Ksenia, help the sick and wayward soldier A., heal him by your prayers from smoking and drunkenness, and give him love."

Interestingly, the fence that kept believers from reaching a place of worship made their prayers more public and permanent. Instead of praying silently or aloud over a lit candle in the chapel, Ksenia's devotees wrote and etched their

requests permanently into the fence. Today the chapel is open to the public during certain hours, but it remains customary to leave letters addressed to Ksenia in crags in the wall when the building is closed. Residents of other cities also send letters, cementing Ksenia's reputation as a saint who cares about intimate worries and responds to written requests as much as to ones voiced in person. It is even possible to submit prayer requests through a website maintained by Ksenia's devotees. In her openness to contemporary concerns and modern forms of communication, Saint Ksenia appeals to a group of believers whose numbers have grown through the Soviet period: an urban, educated person living in cramped spaces and worrying about questions of forming a family, pursuing an education, and regaining or maintaining health. Ksenia's popularity shows that there is demand for such a mundane face of the church.

2

Czech Dissident
Zdeněk Mlynář's Memoir

MICHAEL LONG

In 1971, Adolf Müller and Bedřich Utitz founded Index, a publishing enterprise for Czech exile literature and tamizdat based in Cologne, West Germany. Index published approximately 1,200 titles until it ceased operations in 1990. The company specialized in works by Czech authors forbidden from publishing in Czechoslovakia, including Václav Havel, Pavel Kohout, Ludvík Vaculik, Jiří Gruša, Jaroslav Seifert, Jan Potočka, Ota Filip, Lenka Procházková, and others. Index was well-connected to the underground channels for transferring literature in and out of Czechoslovakia. A network of drivers and couriers aided in the transport of 200–300 copies of each Index title across the German-Czechoslovak border, most often in a modified Citroen.

The edition of *Mráz přichází z Kremlu* depicted here is a 1981 Index edition prepared for the smuggling operation. It measures 3.5 by 2.5 inches and has a simple adhesive binding and chipboard cover. The applied label bears traces of the book's title. *Mráz přichází z Kremlu*, translated literally in English as "frost approaches from the Kremlin," is Zdeněk Mlynář's memoir. The Index edition of the memoir is the first publication of *Mráz* in Czech. The English version, titled *Nightfrost in Prague*, bears the subtitle *The End of Humane Socialism*.

Mlynář (June 22, 1930–April 15, 1997) joined the Communist Party of Czechoslovakia in 1946 at the age of sixteen. From 1951 to 1955, he studied law at Moscow State University, where he befriended fellow classmate Mikhail Sergeevich Gorbachev. Mlynář's experiences in Moscow as a student had a profound impact on his political views and his future career in politics; he recalls that "it was my five years in Moscow that gave rise to my first serious ideological doubts." A reform communist, Mlynář quickly rose to the position of party secretary and became a member of Alexander Dubček's inner circle. Two days after the Warsaw Pact invasion of Czechoslovakia, shortly after midnight on August 21, 1968, Mlynář flew to Moscow with other members of the Czechoslovak government and Central Committee, where he participated in the "talks" between members of the Czechoslovak Communist Party and government, including Dubček, President Ludvík Svoboda, and others, both reform Communists and hard-liners, with members of the Soviet Politburo and Soviet Premier Leonid Brezhnev. After the signing of the Moscow Protocol, which effectively ended the reform era of the Prague Spring and set the agenda for "normalization," Mlynář

resigned his position in 1970 and was soon after expelled from the Communist Party. Thereafter, he worked as a researcher in entomology for the National Museum. Due to harassment by state security services for signing Charter 77, Mlynář emigrated with his family to Austria at the invitation of Austrian Chancellor Bruno Kreisky. Mlynář returned to Prague after the Velvet Revolution and tried his hand at politics. In the 1996 parliamentary elections, Mlynář's party was rejected by voters, after which he returned to Vienna. Mlynář was tenured as a professor of political science at Innsbruck University. He died in 1997.

Mlynář's fly-on-the-wall analysis of intraparty machinations and the character assessments of leading Czech political figures in *Mráz* make it clear that the work had to be published outside Czechoslovakia. The author provides an honest reflection on his own attraction to the ideals of the Soviet model of Marxism-Leninism during his youth and how his understanding changed over time, leading him ultimately to join the reform wing of the party that launched the Prague Spring. Perhaps the most explosive contents of *Mráz* are Mlynář's frank evaluations of the character of party and government functionaries, including Dubček, Svoboda, Gustáv Husák, František Kriegl, and Alois Indra.

3

Communist Anti-Islam Propaganda

JULIE deGRAFFENRIED

Muslims comprised a sizeable religious minority in the Soviet Union, second only to the Orthodox. By the late 1980s, some fifty-four million citizens—approximately 20 percent of the population—belonged to one of the approximately forty nationalities that had adopted Islam. Two-thirds of Muslims lived in the Central Asian republics, with the remaining one-third mostly in the Caucasus and Russia. As of 1942, "official" Islam existed with state permission. Four Spiritual Directorates supervised all working mosques, schools, religious publications, and clerics, the number of which had been radically diminished since prerevolutionary times. Although the law deemed activities outside these registered institutions illegal, unofficial versions of Islam persisted.

This poster, likely from the 1970s, illustrates one of the state's common charges against Islam: the oppression of women. Uneducated, veiled to varying degrees, kept from employment by motherhood and seclusion, Muslim women were viewed as the victims of backward, patriarchal attitudes. Beginning in the 1920s, Communist Party activists launched emancipation efforts, most notoriously with mass, public unveiling ceremonies in Central Asia, in order to weaken traditional authorities and build socialism. A renewed attack on Islam in the postwar era resulted in the dramatic decrease of practices such as veiling, bridewealth (*kalym*), child marriage, and polygamy while female literacy rates increased from 1–2 percent to 97 percent, and women gained legal rights and employment opportunities, particularly in urban areas.

Central News Agency TASS cartoonist and graphic artist Igor Efimovich Sychëv's 64 by 47-centimeter tricolor lithograph suggests that the "woman

Суть его характера видна:
У него имеются два дна.
Сверху—где он развернул газету,
Снизу—где он верен Магомету.

question" was far from resolved. In an inverted pyramid against a cerulean sky, a large suited man holding a newspaper bearing the headline "Women's Emancipation" sits on the back of a domesticated donkey that is being borne on the shoulders of a downcast Muslim woman. Framing this top-heavy column are modern apartment buildings on the left juxtaposed with mosques and crescent-topped minarets on the right. The latter help to identify which faith community Sychëv addresses, as do the prayer beads on the man's wrist and the verse at the bottom of the poster. It reads: "The essence of his character is clear: / He has two sides. / On the surface, where he follows the Party. / Underneath, where he remains loyal to Mohammed." Though the man bears a newspaper lauding gender equality, he is only pretending to be progressive. Because of his beliefs, he has not one but *two* beasts of burden—his animal and his wife. Meant to mock and shame, the poster implies that Muslim women remain oppressed despite Soviet-led advances and that Islam continues to stand in the way of equality and, thus, socialism.

Visual cues indicate the targets of criticism are Uzbek and Tajik men. The man wears a *tupi*, traditional Tajik and Uzbek headwear, while the woman wears a *tupi* and scarf (*rumol*), headgear adopted by Tajik and Uzbek women following the unveiling campaigns of the 1920s. Further, the structures in the bottom right are meant to resemble famous mosques in Bukhara and Samarkand, historic Persian cities located in the Uzbek republic. This is no fluke: the poster takes aim precisely at the most religious and conservative population in Soviet Central Asia.

Despite this specificity, the artist employs two themes common to anti-religious propaganda. First, the believer is "unmasked," revealing that his true allegiance is to faith, not ideology, state, or society. Unmasking of enemies was a longtime convention in the Soviet Union, and one used frequently against believers. Second, modern socialist life and the life of faith are depicted as dichotomous. The separated architectural structures and text intimate one could be either modern and socialist or backward and religious—not both. Reality suggested otherwise.

4

The Siberian Seven

EMILY B. BARAN

Unable to legally register their congregations or to practice their specific form of Christianity, Soviet Pentecostals petitioned for the right to emigrate abroad to countries that would allow them greater religious freedom. By the late 1970s, the Pentecostal emigration movement encompassed thousands of believers and began to attract interest from sympathetic western audiences, who also lobbied for emigration rights for Soviet Jews. The Soviet government, however, rejected nearly all emigration applications from Pentecostals. Believers who refused to abandon their efforts faced significant harassment and discrimination. Some lost their jobs; others lost custody of their children. At least a few were arrested and imprisoned in labor camps or psychiatric hospitals.

The Vashchenko family from the mining settlements near the Siberian city of Chernogorsk suffered particularly hard under these conditions. Augustina and Peter Vashchenko had fourteen children and lost custody of their eldest daughters after refusing to send them to a school where they would be taught atheism. Both parents spent time behind bars after making repeated journeys to Moscow to seek emigration assistance at the American Embassy. In 1978, six members of the Vashchenko family, along with two individuals from the Chmykhalov family, again traveled to Moscow for information. This time, one of the Vashchenko sons was arrested at the gate while the rest made it inside embassy grounds. The families decided not to leave until they were granted emigration abroad. After spending weeks in the consular waiting area, they were given their own room in the embassy basement. Their prolonged stay became a source of curiosity and concern among western Christians, who dubbed them "the Siberian Seven."

Months, then years, passed without any resolution. American officials could do little to help the families without Soviet intervention, and Soviet officials saw no need to address the situation at all. Stuck in limbo, the Siberian Seven criticized both governments for their seeming unwillingness to grant them freedom abroad. Increasingly desperate, some of the Vashchenko women began a hunger strike in late 1981 to draw attention to their plight. Within weeks, the health of one of the hunger strikers, Lida Vashchenko, deteriorated to a dangerous degree. Embassy staff made the decision to transfer her to a Soviet hospital outside embassy walls. This photograph was taken in January 1982 as officials escorted Lida to Botkin Hospital in Moscow. The hunger strike brought newfound media attention to the Siberian Seven. From her hospital bed, Lida wrote a letter to her growing supporters to thank them for championing her cause. Keston News Service circulated the letter, which read in part: "Since my family, beginning with my grandfather, has never belonged to the Communist system, why now in front of the world is it necessary to struggle with us or to prevent us from emigrating, revealing the powerlessness of the atheistic system to re-educate such a small group as my family?"

With her hospitalization, Lida's hunger strike ended. Rather than rejoin her family back in the embassy, Lida returned home to her brothers and sisters. While the hunger strike did not immediately yield results, Lida's return to Chernogorsk ultimately broke the stalemate. From her hometown, she renewed her emigration paperwork with authorities. In early 1983, Soviet officials finally let her leave the Soviet Union. When the remaining members of the Siberian Seven confirmed that she had safely landed abroad, they agreed to return to Chernogorsk and successfully petitioned to emigrate as well. It was a rare victory in the Pentecostal emigration movement. Large-scale emigration would have to wait until the transformative leadership of Mikhail Gorbachev and the collapse of the Soviet Union.

5

The Great White Brotherhood

ZOE KNOX

The Keston Archive includes material on a countless number of religious groups active in the former communist bloc, some long established and well known and others relatively recent and largely obscure. The latter includes the Great White Brotherhood (*Velikoe beloe bratstvo*), an apocalyptic movement based in Kiev, Ukraine, which emerged in the early 1990s and gained wide, if fleeting, notoriety across Belarus, Russia, and Ukraine.

This eclectic collection of documents includes a letter from Aleksandr, a twenty-three-year-old Christian from Rostov-on-Don in Russia. Written in halting English, the letter is undated and to "dear friends." We can only guess, given its preservation in the archive, that Aleksandr meant to address Keston personnel. He warns of the activities of a "terrible sect" he calls the "Great White Community," writing, "Often ministries [ministers] of Great White Community preach their teachings in the main street (Bolshaya Sadovaya Str.) in the center of our city. They wear white robes. Their teaching is very heretical."

He enclosed a leaflet published by the Brotherhood bearing striking images of its founder-leaders, Marina Tsvigun and Yuri Krivonogov. They called themselves Maria Devi Christos or "The Messiah" and Youann Swami or "The High Priest." The leaflet reveals a syncretic belief system called "Iusmalos," an amalgam of its leaders' names. It warns of an impending apocalypse that will purge the world of sinners and identifies Kiev as the "New Jerusalem." The other documents are more mundane: articles on the Brotherhood in the *Daily Telegraph* (a British newspaper), and *Izvestia* and *Komsomolskaya Pravda* (Russian newspapers), and a press survey compiled by the Radio Free Europe/Radio Liberty Research Institute, all from mid-1993.

The Great White Brotherhood aroused intense media scrutiny later that year when sensationalist articles reported that it had 150,000 followers and that a mass suicide would take place when they descended on Kiev. Tsvigun planned to crucify herself and prophesied that the world would end on November 14, 1993. Four days prior to this date, her white-robed followers entered the Cathedral of Saint Sophia, an eleventh-century Orthodox cathedral of great architectural, historical, and national significance in the center of Kiev. Tsvigun intended to sermonize inside the Cathedral. Clashes between Orthodox believers and members of the Brotherhood ensued. Riot police arrived and were only able to restore order after violent confrontations with members. About sixty followers were arrested during the fracas as were another 800 in Kiev. The figure of 150,000 was greatly exaggerated. Tsvigun and Krivonogov were sentenced to prison. Following her release several years later, Tsvigun continued to teach as a guru, but she is largely unknown today.

Taken together, these materials reveal the intense interest in this now obscure syncretic movement, the type of literature disseminated by the Brotherhood across the region, and how unsettling the new religious pluralism was for some Christians, like Aleksandr. They also demonstrate the efforts of Keston personnel to keep abreast of the rapidly changing religious landscape. This was a challenging task given the resurgence of traditional faiths, the emergence of underground communities, the rise of new religious movements, and the influx of western Christian missionaries across the region. These developments were covered almost obsessively by the Russian press, and western newspapers followed suit, making the information available to analysts of religion in the former Soviet Union almost overwhelming. At the same time as this flourishing of religious activity and explosion of information, donations to Keston dried up as the charity's core mission—to give voice to persecuted believers behind the Iron Curtain—seemed moribund.

6

Sir John Lawrence,
Early Keston Advocate

XENIA DENNEN

Sir John Lawrence (1907–1999) loved to tell a wartime story about his sheepskin coat: he was on his way by sea to Archangel with two other "official representatives of British Culture," as they are called in this section's photograph of John (far right), taken in 1942, whereupon he was torpedoed off Spitsbergen and found himself in the water. A briefcase of secret papers, containing weights to make it sink, in fact floated, and his sheepskin coat emerged with a large section ripped off that he felt sure indicated that the torpedo had passed between his legs.

John was on his way as press attaché to the USSR where he was to set up and then edit a new publication, *The British Ally* (*Britanskii soiuznik*), the only uncensored publication to appear between the reigns of Lenin and Gorbachev. John's wartime experience led him to devote his life and writing to Russia; he was shocked at the treatment of his many Russian friends by Stalin and came to see that the defense of human rights and religious liberty were essential. Michael Bourdeaux described him as his "guiding light in the founding of Keston Institute." He served as Keston's first chairman and then president for over fourteen years, during which the world came to acknowledge Keston's work on religious liberty in the Soviet bloc.

For me, too, John was a guiding light. When I was asked to found Keston's journal, *Religion in Communist Lands*, in 1973, I always showed him my editorial and got advice on improvements. "You will catch or lose your reader in the first sentence," he would say. "Cut out the adjectives and put in more verbs." I also

OFFICIAL REPRESENTATIVES OF BRITISH CULTURE,
ARCHANGEL, 1942

George Reavey: Barry Cornwell: John Lawrence

travelled with John during the 1970s on trips to the Soviet Union and met many of his wartime friends. He likened living in Russia to "swimming in glue" and prided himself on how he could deal with Russian officialdom. "You must lose your temper at the right moment," he explained, and as a result his travelling companions managed to see something off the beaten track, some wonderful Orthodox church that was not usually shown to the public. While a convinced ecumenist, John felt drawn to the spirituality of the Russian Orthodox Church. He had a strong sense of the communion of saints and would say, "We have an open edge," meaning that we were linked to our neighbor and to those who had gone before us.

John had ideas on how the Soviet Union could be reformed. In an essay entitled "If I were Tsar" that he marked "not for publication" and dated July 1, 1977, he advised that "an evolution of the present Soviet system provides the best hope both for Russia and for her neighbours. Another revolution would be likely to make everything worse." Collectivization of agriculture should end, and those who worked the land should be allowed to own and work it in their own way. He did not recommend privatization and believed the Soviet administration should be decentralized. He wanted the rule of law introduced, the KGB curbed, and the Lubyanka torn down, but he did not recommend introducing a multiparty system or debunking Lenin straightaway. All should happen gradually, including the abolition of censorship.

In his book *Russians Observed*, John admitted to having ambiguous feelings about Russia, for "either you hate it or you love it, and more probably both." In his case love, I think, predominated, and his insight was remarkable—some would say even prophetic. Michael Bourdeaux remembers him pronouncing, "There's no substance in it! Communism will collapse like a house of cards, and I shall live to see it!" And indeed he did.

7

Father Aleksandr Men's *Son of Man*

WALLACE L. DANIEL

Son of Man (*Syn Chelovecheskii*) is a foundational book in Father Aleksandr Men's life and writings. Perhaps Russia's most outstanding pastor in the second half of the twentieth century, Men (1935–1990) served the Russian Orthodox Church during some of the most tumultuous years of the Soviet era. Ordained in 1960 at the age of twenty-five, Men spent his entire adult life as a village priest in several small parishes outside Moscow, where he attracted large numbers of the Russian intelligentsia. He had the unusual ability to preach and speak effectively across all educational levels in Soviet society. It was this gift that made him widely known among people, young and old, who were searching for life's meaning beyond the Marxist ideological paradigm favored by the regime. Among such people, Men's *Son of Man* became a key text.

During his teenage years, Aleksandr Men recognized the need for a straightforward, inspiring, deeply researched, and well-written account of the life of Jesus. It would have to appeal to a people who were largely ignorant of the Gospels and who were taught that biblical teachings were mythological concoctions, possessing little meaning to a society based on rationality and science. He began work on the original manuscript in the mid-1950s, continually rewriting the text and researching newly discovered texts. He completed the manuscript in 1968 when he served in the village parish of Tarasovka, thirty miles north of Moscow, having witnessed at first hand the desire of his parishioners for such a book. Because Soviet censorship prohibited such religious works, he sent it abroad, where it was published in 300 copies by the small Brussels press, La Vie avec Dieu (*Zhizn's Bogom*), and under the pen name of Andrei Bogoliubov. The book was smuggled back into Russia and extensively distributed through samizdat.

The copy of *Son of Man* held in the Keston Archive is the second printing of the original 1968 edition. The book includes the same illustrations and appendixes, including the important essay "Myth or Reality?" ("*Mif ili deistvitel'nost'?*"), in which Men challenged the Soviet mythologists' claim that Jesus never existed. *Son of Man* attempted to show how Jesus differed from all other prophetic voices of the ancient world. Men presented him not only as a teacher but as the "Incarnation of the Living God." Christ offered a new way of looking at human beings, as containing a divine and creative presence. *Son of Man* portrayed Christ as the "Liberator."

Not all Russian readers responded positively to *Son of Man*. But large numbers of people who read his book found it compelling. It made them see the world differently than before. Written in a narrative style, it placed the reader in concrete situations set against the background of sacred events. It was a signal accomplishment. "He translated the gospel stories into the idiom of the modern Russian people," said his fellow priest, Father Gleb Yakunin. "He tried to bring the Gospels to the people in a language they could understand. That was his foremost mission in life."

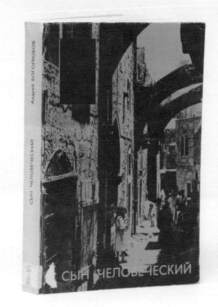

Although not officially published in Russia until after Father Aleksandr's murder in 1990, to date the book has sold more than one million copies. As the Sinyavsky-Daniel trial in 1965–1966 opened up the road to the dissident movement, the publication and distribution of *Son of Man* opened up the road to the Church and to traditions that had long been submerged.

8

The Trial of Aida Skripnikova

MICHAEL BOURDEAUX

In 1969, I unwrapped a soft parcel and out of it tumbled a document, the like of which I never saw before or since. We had other transcripts of the trials of Russian Baptists, but this was not like them. It was written in ballpoint pen on eleven sheets—literally bedsheets, cut into long narrow strips, subdivided into twenty-two numbered sections. They were covered by faultless handwriting, headed "Legal case regarding Aida Mikhailovna Skripnikova," and reconstructed her trial, in many passages verbatim.

I understood that this painstaking work had been undertaken to facilitate its transport out of the Soviet Union. Finnish citizens could easily acquire short-term visas to visit Leningrad or Tallinn. A young lady had wrapped this around her middle so that it could not be detected at the frontier except in the unlikely event of a strip search.

Among the hostile "public" admitted to such trials, an anonymous sympathizer had managed to secrete herself and—with incredible bravery—take detailed notes on the proceedings and somehow evade surveillance on leaving the courtroom. From these it was possible to reconstruct the trial and transcribe the substance into this format.

Aida's name was already known in the West and, through Keston's later publicity, she became a symbol of the persecution of the Russian Baptists in the 1960s. She was born in 1941 and was still only twenty-six at the time of this second arrest. Her father had been shot as a pacifist when she was still an infant. Her mother brought up her and her brother as Christians. Then tragedy struck: her brother fell ill and died, which deeply affected her.

She determined that she must do something to stand publicly for her faith. On New Year's Eve 1961, she stood on a street corner on Leningrad's Nevsky Prospekt and handed greetings cards to passersby. She found postcards of a painting by Claude Lorrain depicting a harbor at sunrise. She interpreted this as a Christian symbol of a new life and wrote her own poem on several copies. This read, in part, "What answer will you give your Creator? . . . Answer this question while light remains."

She was soon arrested, interrogated, put in a psychiatric hospital (which found her completely normal), and briefly imprisoned, which made her all the more determined to spread the good news of her faith. This led to attacks against her in the press and eventually the trial of which these strips of bedsheets are the transcript. The trial began on July 11, 1967.

The brutality and intimidation of a defenseless young woman are there, but more interesting is the fearless way in which (unusually for such trials, of which there were many) a succession of witnesses unanimously testified to her integrity and honesty. Their words are recorded. Every Soviet trial theoretically guaranteed the right of the defendant to a "last word." Aida had been denied the right to a defense lawyer, but her final words are recorded. Part of what she said was this: "Believers cannot promise to fulfil a law which forbids them to talk about God and which forbids parents to bring up their children in the faith. . . . No Christian mother or father will accept a law which orders them to bring up their children as atheists."

Her sentence was three years of imprisonment, but on release she continued to work openly for her faith.

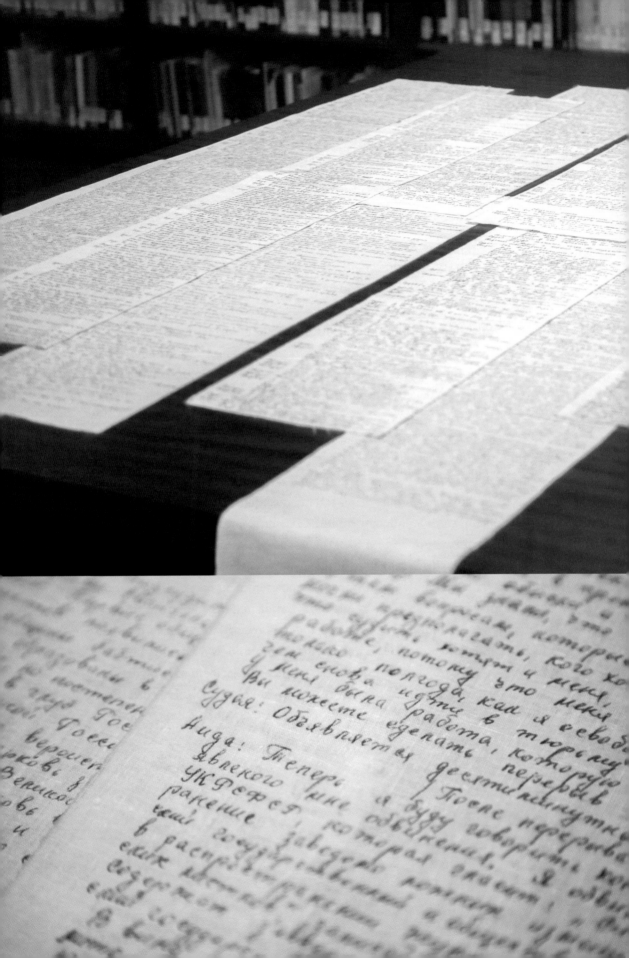

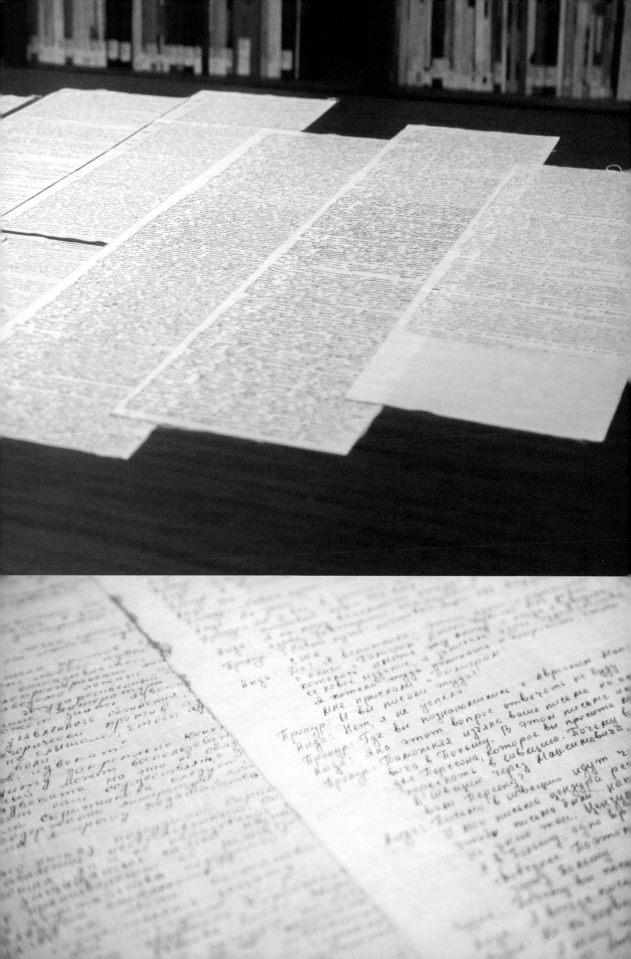

9

International Intervention for Romanian Prisoner of Conscience

ALINA URS

On the morning of April 9, 1982, more than fifty men from the Romanian Mili-
tia and Securitate came to Dorel Catarama's home in Oituz, Romania, and ran-
sacked his house for fourteen hours straight: they knocked holes in the walls,
tore up the wooden floor, pulled out grapevines from his garden. All they found
was ten dozen eggs, thirty kilos of cornmeal, a kilo of meat, and three boxes of
soda. Without anything else at hand, they decided to arrest him on charges of
overstocking food. In a folder located in the Keston Archive, one can find the
trial transcripts, letters, handwritten notes, photographs, and smuggled documents telling the story of Dorel Catarama's imprisonment and the fierce campaign to free him.

Dorel Cataramă, then thirty years old, was married, had one child, and was a
model employee at the factory where he worked as a tailor. But since his youth,
he had been in trouble with the authorities because of his religion. He was a
Seventh-Day Adventist in a totalitarian state where working on a Saturday was
a must. Moreover, his father and brother had recently received asylum in the
United States. This prompted a high-ranking officer of the local secret police to
present Dorel Cataramă with an ultimatum: collaboration or prison. But Dorel
refused to betray his family and friends. His arrest was nonetheless shocking for
his entire family, and his mother, wife, and sister desperately tried to find out the
charges against Dorel, only to be threatened with arrest themselves.

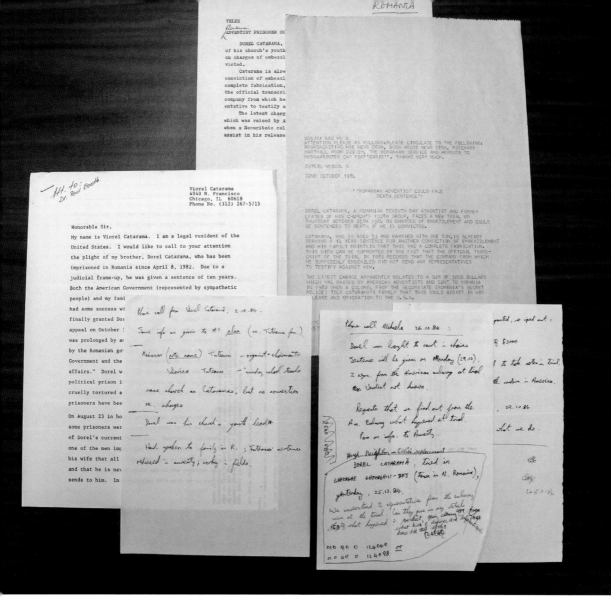

Realizing the shortcomings with the charge of overstocking food, authorities started to build an embezzlement case, accusing Cataramă of stealing money from two state companies where he previously worked. Aware of the consequences, the directors of both companies issued excellent character references for Dorel, denying any wrongdoing on his part. The Securitate, plotting another accusation, told his family to pay the equivalent of $3,000 to set him free. With the help of Adventist communities in the United States, his brother Viorel raised the money and wired it to Romania. This resulted in Dorel being charged with illegally possessing foreign currency. In the first of his three trials, he was sentenced to ten years in prison. In 1983, the sentence was prolonged to fourteen years and all his possessions were confiscated, leaving his family in poverty. In subsequent years, Dorel's location was often unknown to his relatives, visits were denied for months in a row, and reports emerged that he was being starved and beaten.

The campaign for his release was led by Viorel Cataramă, who got in contact with Keston College in the autumn of 1984. From that point onward, Keston contributed by gathering and forwarding information and documents between parties, providing organizations such as Amnesty International with verified data. The Keston News Service published updates, helping convince the West of Cataramă's innocence. In itself, Keston's involvement became a means of constant pressure against the communist authorities in Romania. After two more years, the impact of this campaign could no longer be ignored. The Cataramă case was brought up by U.S. representatives during talks about granting Romania most-favored-nation status, after which President Nicolae Ceauşescu personally ordered his release from prison. In September 1986, Dorel Cataramă said that his prayers had been answered. After what felt not like four but forty years, he was reunited with his family in Chicago.

10

Council of Prisoners' Relatives

APRIL L. FRENCH

This image shows an October 1975 "Message" to Soviet leaders Brezhnev, Podgorny, and Kosygin from Aleksandra "Shura" Kozorezova (1936–2006), who notifies the recipients that she has sent a declaration to Amnesty International concerning violations of the human rights of her imprisoned husband and her family. She enclosed the Amnesty International declaration within the original letter, both of which were then reprinted in volume 27 of the samizdat publication *Bulletin of the Council of the Relatives of Evangelical Christian-Baptist Prisoners of the USSR*. In the declaration to Amnesty International, Kozorezova cites the Helsinki Accords (signed a few months earlier) and enumerates the arbitrary ways her husband, family, and coreligionists had been treated by Soviet officials.

Keston College personnel called the organization that illegally published the *Bulletin* the Council of Prisoners' Relatives (CPR). Established in 1965, CPR was the longest-standing, uninterrupted human rights organization that was run entirely from within the Soviet Union. CPR, which published 143 distinct editions of the *Bulletin* from 1971 to 1987, was established and led by women. In the 1970s, all editions of the CPR *Bulletin* were reproduced via mimeograph. Each *Bulletin* contained reproductions of letters sent from various Baptist believers (individuals and congregations) to authorities in the USSR and to international entities. The Keston Archive and a few other archives in the world contain some of the original letters that were reproduced within the *Bulletin*.

The author of these documents, Shura Kozorezova, was the mother of ten children and the wife of Aleksei Kozorezov, who led unregistered Evangelical

Генеральному Секретарю ЦК КПСС
Брежневу Л.И.
Председателю Президиума Верховно-
го Совета СССР Подгорному Н.В.
Председателю Совета Министров
СССР Косыгину А.Н.

Копия: Совету родственников узников,
осужденных за Слово Божие

от Козорезовой Александры Тимоф
прож. в г.Ворошиловграде- 47 по
ул. Оборонной № 92.

СООБЩЕНИЕ

Считаю себя обязанной поставить в известность о том, что мною послано заявление в Международную амнистию. Я, верующая евангельско-баптистского испове-дания, имею 10 несовершеннолетних детей.

Мой муж, Козорезов Алексей Тимофеевич, тоже христианин, второй раз отбывает срок наказания за свое убеждение в искреннюю веру в Бога. Находится в данное время в г.Омске, п/я УХ 16/7. Вся наша семья до 1975г. тоже жила в г.Омске.

Не один раз мною писались в различные инстанции всевозможные письма, жалобы, заявления с просьбой прекратить преследование нашей семьи, освободить незаконно осужденного мужа, но преследование усиливалось. После моего заявления, посланного Вам в 1971 г. на съезд КПСС, мой муж был арестован.

После заявления жен узников христианок г.Омска, посланного к Вам же нас в доме была произведена прокуратурой Ленинского р-на г.Омска в 1974г. обыск. А меня на глазах детей за руки и за ноги уволокли в прокуратуру на допрос.

Но на мою жалобу к Вам об этом беззаконии мне был дан ответ, что со мною поступили правильно, по закону, нарушений со стороны органов прокуратуры не было.

И много других заявлений было послано к Вам. Но реакция с Вашей стороны была всегда отрицательная.

Поэтому на этот раз я решила обратиться в международную амнистию. Заявление, посланное туда прилагаю.

октябрь 1975г.   Козорезова

28

В Международную амнистию
Советскому Правительству
Совету родственников узников,
осужденных за Слово Божие в СССР

Копия: от Козорезовой Александры Тим
прож. г. Ворошиловград-47 СССР
ул. Оборонная 92, октябрь 1975г.

ЗАЯВЛЕНИЕ

Первого августа 1975г. в г. Хельсинки был подписан договор между странами мира о правах человека. В лице своих представителей подписывающих договор, страны давали обещание друг другу уважать права человека, независимо от нации, расы, пола, религиозных убеждений. В числе подписавших была и наша страна.

В Советском Союзе нас, последователей ЕХБ, последние десятилетие жестоко преследуют за то, что мы хотим жить по Евангелию, исполняя заповеди нашего Господа Иисуса Христа.

Мой муж Козорезов Алексей Тимофеевич уже второй раз лишен свободы. Первый раз он был осужден в 1966 году и приговорен Омским областном к 3-м годам лишения свободы с содержанием в тюрьме. Этот срок он провел в застенках Владимирской тюрьмы. 2 раза в год по получаса мы могли с ним увидеться и поговорить в присутствии надзирателя. Один Бог мог укрепить его слабеющие силы и помочь ему перенести все трудности, тюремного режима. Затем 2 года на свободе. Но эта "свобода" для искренне верующего человека мало отличается от жизни в тюрьме или лагере. Постоянные преследования, слежки, угрозы, штрафы по 50 руб. за посещение молитвенных собраний. Еще и до сих пор не удержан полностью 50-ти рублевый штраф на судоремонтном заводе г. Омска, где работал в то время мой муж, не успели.

В 1971 году 14 мая он был вновь арестован и 23 июля этого года Омским областном приговорен к 5-ти годам лишения свободы с содержанием в лагере строгого режима. Снова разлука с семьей. 10 малолетних детей остались без отца. Семья без кормильца. Снова на мои женские плечи легло непосильное бремя одиночества в воспитании детей, в их материальном обеспечении. 7 сыновей растут без отца, да и дочерям он также нужен. Дети ждали и не пропускали возможности побывать у отца на свидании, которые не так уж часты. Были случаи, когда нам пообещают свидание, мы приедем все, а нам по известным

29

ным причинам свидание переносят на 2-3 недели позже или вообще отменяют. Как это действует на психику детей, никого не интересует.

Муж отбывает срок наказания в г. Омске п/я УХ 16/7. Семья тогда тоже жила в г. Омске. Уже пятый год идет, как отец отнят у детей. Дети подросли, но все равно любовь к отцу у них не угасла, а с их возрастом еще больше возросла и они с еще большим желанием стремятся увидеть отца.

В данное время семья наша выехала из г. Омска в г. Ворошиловград. Муж находится по прежнему адресу в г. Омске. За 4г. и 4 м-ца у него не было нарушения режима, производственный план он ежемесячно перевыполнял. Работой его начальство было довольно. Нам разрешили иметь дополнительное свидание с семьей на 3 суток. Теперь мы уже не в одном городе с ним и, конечно, все, как это было прежде, не смогли приехать на свидание. Я поехала с 2-мя меньшими.

В г. Омске 19 лет девушка-христианка Савченко Лена, отец которой за упование на Бога дважды отбывал срок, имела большое желание увидеться с братом в Господе и отцом по возрасту моим мужем А.Т. Ее желание мы принесли к Господу нашему. И вот совершенно неожиданно ее пропустили на свидание, причем за одну из наших дочерей. Но на 2-ой день, когда Лена ушла от нас, ее приглашали в оперчасть, обыскали там /выдали приказ начальника оперчасти обыскать/ за то шовника! Лену допрашивали, сфотографировали без ее согласия. Лена не отвечала на вопросы, ей угрожали посадить в клетку. А когда она осталась наедине с начальником оперчасти Турченко, то он, сжав кулаки, сказал: "Вот как ежи бы, так ты и кровью бы зашлась!" Но он прав таких не имел, о чем сам сказал тут же. Теперь на Лену хотят подвести по административную комиссию за "связь с заключенным" Оказывается есть такая ст. послушал нач. оперчасти колонии № г. Омска.

Наше свидание было прервано. А за то, что мой муж Козорезов А.Т. не предал Лену, не заявил начальству, что к нему пришла повторница девушка, его посадили в штрафную изолятор на 15суток. Где голые нары, сам полураздетый, камера холодная. Полуголодный - вдень кусочек хлеба и стакан воды. За что? Лена нам не посторонняя, она подруга нашей дочери, выросшая вместе с нашей дочерью и сама нам, как дочь.

Кроме того нач. оперчасти сказал мне, что у моего мужа есть Евангелие и что они у него найдут его, а мужа моего снова накажут за чтение запрещенной для лагеря литературы. Значит Евангелие - это запрещенная литература. Но я нигде такого закона не читала, я считаю, что это произвол, даже попирание прав верующих, когда запрещают под страхом наказания читать Евангелие и Библию. Органы КГБ г. Омска заинтересованы в том, чтобы Козорезову по освобождению дать надзор и они выискивают причины, чтобы сделать его нарушителем режима. Я не уверена, что в после-

30

ние месяцы перед освобождением не будет сделано покушение на его здоровье, жизнь.

Сегодня, кратко описав положение моего мужа и семьи, я прошу Вас ходатайствовать перед нашим правительством об освобождении Козорезова А.Т., как незаконно и фальшиво осужденного по ст. ст. 142 ч2, 190, 227 УК РСФСР.

Мой муж искренне верующий христианин, стремящийся исполнить волю Божию во всем, служащий Господу и церкви Его. Чтобы изолировать его от верующих и своих собственных детей, ему, как и всем другим осужденным верующим, сфабриковали уголовное дело по выше названным статьям. Обвинения по этим ст. не только не подходят к верующим по их убеждениям, но даже оскорбляют чувства верующих, не говоря уже о том, что права наши, как верующих, попираются.

Я, многодетная мать, прошу Вас, как международную организацию, немедленно вникнуть в вопрос о преследовании верующих в нашей стране и ходатайствовать перед нашим правительством о немедленном освобождении всех узников-христиан, осужденных по различным несоответствующим для них статьям.

Вас и даже нас пытаются убедить в том, что осужденные узники-христиане совершили преступление против закона и осуждены не за убеждение. Но почитайте, изучите обвинительные заключения наших братьев и сестер, их приговора и Вы легко убедитесь в том, что братья наши и сестры искренне и самоотверженно проповедуют Христа распятого среди детей, молодежи, взрослых. Этому нас обязывает вера Евангелия. Итак, идите по всему миру и проповедуйте Евангелие всей твари /Марк.16:15/. "...Итак, идите научите все народы..." /Мф. 28:19/ и другие места.

Как мы можем поступить иначе?

Прочитав обвинительные заключения и приговора наших братьев, Вы увидите в том, что они искренне совершали служение в церкви, порой оставив дома свои ради Господа и этому нас обязывает Евангелие.

А разве то, что нашим братьям и сестрам узникам не разрешают прийти посетить их же единоверцам, прийти совершить вечерю Господню /это необходимая заповедь для христиан/, не разрешают иметь Евангелие, Библию, больше того, считают эти книги запрещенными.

Я еще раз убедительно прошу Вас ходатайствовать об освобождении как моего мужа Козорезова, ныне отбывающего срок в г. Омске, п/я УХ 16/7, так и всех остальных узников-христиан, среди них большое количество таких же многодетных отцов, как и мой муж. Их жены и дети также жестокостью приговоров лишены кормильцев-отцов.

После этого письма к Вам меня могут обвинить в клевете и привлечь к ответственности. Но я боюсь Бога прежде всего, а потому презираю клевету.

Октябрь 1975 год   Козорезова.

31

Christian-Baptist (ECB) congregations in Omsk, Russia, and Voroshilovgrad, Ukraine. Aleksei spent over twelve years in prisons or camps between 1966 and 1986, leaving Shura to raise her family. At the time of this writing, Aleksei was in the fourth year of his second prison term, a five-year sentence. From 1966 to 1978, Shura was an active member of CPR. She became its chairwoman in 1979, leading the organization until 1987, when the final edition of the *Bulletin* was published (all ECB prisoners having been released by then).

Shura was a force of nature, but she regularly wrote about how helpless she and her children felt. In her letters, she demonstrates the courage to stand up to Soviet authorities in order to petition for her family's and coreligionists' rights. She also describes her family's plight in desperate terms. The varied language and tones within these two documents—equal portions strength and desperation—is representative of thousands of similar letters sent to Soviet and international officials by ECB believers and widely distributed by CPR.

One cannot help but notice the gendered complexity within the letters Shura and others write. On the one hand, Shura is a leading member of an organization run by women that appealed insistently for the rights of religious freedom for their coreligionists (mostly men). On the other hand, a traditionalist evangelical view of gendered norms is apparent. Shura was highly educated, having nearly completed medical school in the Soviet Union (she left as a result of her faith). Yet, not being allowed to actually work in the healthcare field but only in menial jobs as the mother of ten children, including one with special needs, Shura found it difficult to run her household without the support of her "breadwinning" husband. Many ECB women faced similar challenges, negotiating the complexities of their faith, their family, and a society run by an explicitly antireligious government.

11

The Pope's Historic Visit to Poland

ZOE KNOX

Pope John Paul II's nine-day visit to his native Poland in June 1979 was only his second foreign trip as Pope. He eventually travelled extensively during his pontificate (including nine pastoral visits to Poland, more than to any other country), but this one was of particular significance. It was the first papal visit to a communist country. It sent an unambiguous message that the Vatican would not be complicit in the geopolitical tensions that divided Roman Catholics in its European heartlands and more broadly, the global Catholic community. The visit also defied the efforts of the Polish United Workers' Party (PUWP) to minimize Catholicism's influence over Poles and to marginalize Catholic clergy. It thus mounted a profound challenge to communism's ideological monopoly in Poland, one that had far-reaching consequences.

These photographs show John Paul II addressing an audience of students from the Catholic University of Lublin (KUL). Through a sea of crosses, we see cardinals, priests, and nuns gathered to hear him speak and journalists and photographers documenting the occasion. The gilded statues adorning the church contrast with the simple wooden crosses held by the KUL students. In the first photograph, the Pope is watched with intense interest by the crowd. In the second, his address presumably over, the individuals in the shot look joyful and relaxed. Handwritten notes on the backs of both photographs show that they were taken on June 6, the midpoint of his visit. The location is Częstochowa, home to the Pauline monastery of Jasna Góra, a popular pilgrimage site known to Catholics worldwide. It houses the famous Black Madonna painting. The photographs were taken by different photographers. We can possibly see one of them in the more distant image, to the Pope's right.

In October 1978, less than a year before this visit, Cardinal Karol Józef Wojtyła was elected Pope John Paul II, becoming the first non-Italian pontiff since the sixteenth century. The Pope had a long-standing connection with KUL as an instructor (it has since been renamed John Paul II Catholic University of Lublin). KUL had the distinction of being the only Catholic university in the Soviet bloc. It attracted students from around Poland who rejected the tropes of standard Marxist higher education. The Pope must have known many of the faculty in the audience that day.

The existing link between the Catholic Church and Polish anti-communist movements was strengthened by the Pope's visit. Most notably it boosted the morale of workers in the dockyards of Poland's Baltic Sea ports. In 1980, Solidarity (*Solidarność*), an independent labor union, was formed under the leadership of Lech Wałęsa. Its very existence challenged the legitimacy of the PUWP, which claimed to represent the workers. Catholic clergy were involved with Solidarity from the first, conducting mass for striking workers and lending support to their struggle. Although driven underground by communist authorities, Solidarity gathered strength over the next decade and was eventually victorious in elections in June 1989. Wałęsa became president the following year. These developments were closely watched by opposition forces in neighboring communist countries.

The Pope's 1979 visit was a turning point in Polish history and in the course of the Cold War. It not only encouraged the formation of Solidarity but prompted ordinary Poles, who turned out in their millions to see him, to demand that communist authorities respect human rights and dignities. They were empowered and emboldened by the pontiff's calls for courage. The visit is widely understood to mark the beginning of the end of communism in Poland, of the Soviet Empire, and of Soviet-style communism itself.

12

Tat'iana Goricheva's Letter of Support for a Fellow Dissident

ELIZABETH SKOMP

On behalf of the members of the Leningrad Religio-Philosophical Seminar, Tat'iana Goricheva drafted this statement of support for fellow religious dissident Vladimir Poresh in late 1979 following his arrest. Goricheva, a prominent figure in Leningrad unofficial culture during the Brezhnev era, together with her then-husband, poet Viktor Krivulin, and their friend Evgenii Pazukhin, led the Religio-Philosophical Seminar and produced the samizdat journal *37*. Goricheva was also the intellectual leader of the women's independent religious club Mariia that published a samizdat journal of the same name. The Keston Archive's holdings include numerous issues of *37* and other materials related to the Religio-Philosophical Seminar and the Mariia group.

Poresh was one of the leaders of the Moscow-based Christian Seminar founded by Aleksandr Ogorodnikov, and he directed the group's activities in Leningrad. As Goricheva notes in the statement of support, Poresh was arrested on August 1, 1979, for violating Article 70 (also known as the Anti-Soviet Agitation and Propaganda law) of the Criminal Code of the RSFSR through his work on *Community* (*Obshchina*), the samizdat publication of the Christian Seminar.

The expression of concern and sympathy for Poresh by the members of the Leningrad Religio-Philosophical Seminar was an important way of establishing a connection between their group and the Christian Seminar. Though the Leningrad-based group in its meetings and writings included a wider range of voices and viewpoints than did those of the Christian Seminar, the two groups

Владимир Пореш
арестован 1 августа 1979 г. До сих пор находится под следствием
(грозит расправа по 70 ст. статье)
Вл. Пореш — организатор (вместе с Ал. Огородниковым) московского
семинара по проблемам христианского Возрождения в
России. Семинар существует в Москве с 1375 г.
Семинар издаёт журнал "Община". Первый номер
этого религиозно-философского и художественного
журнала был полностью изъят так и не дойдя до
читателя. Второй номер получил большой отклик в широких кругах русской
интеллигенции. Вл. Пореш был арестован перед
выпуском в свет 3 его номера журнала
"Община".

      Для Владимира христианство было религиозным
воплощением и подвига. Он понимал, как ответственно
положение христианина в современном мире. Он
говорил о необходимости создавать христианскую
культуру, христианскую науку, христианскую обществен-
ность. "Видеть крест — принять Дух"—
так появилось одно у отца Владимира. Он был
готов к жертве и ко всему, достойно перенести выпав-
шие на его долю испытание. И всё же мы обращаемся к вам,
мы просим всех христиан молиться за Владимира,
мы просим поднять голос протеста в его защиту.
Владимир нужен нам как проповедник и организатор,
как мыслитель и воспитатель. Мы живём в то
время, когда христианство в России становится реальной,
формирующей силой, когда на каждом шагу выполняет-
ся евангельское слово "Жатва многа, а делателей мало."
Вл. Пореш — один из самых ревностных делателей христианского
Возрождения в России. Помогите нам, помогите ему!
Помогите А. Огородникову, которому грозит второй срок.

            От ленинградского религиозно-философ-
      ского семинара —
                  Татьяна Горичева

saw themselves as essentially similar. The statement also implicitly acknowledges Poresh's leadership of the Christian Seminar in Leningrad, his contributions to *37*, and his role as a bridge between the two groups.

Goricheva's handwritten statement focuses on *Community* and its fraught publication history; the first issue had been seized by the KGB and thus did not reach its intended readership. She emphasizes Poresh's understanding of "the responsibility of being a Christian in the contemporary world" and the sacrifice that such a role might require. His article "Give blood and receive the spirit," which appeared in the second issue of *Community*, explores these ideas in more depth.

The statement of support was published in a slightly different form in *Russian Thought (Russkaia Mysl')* on December 27, 1979, signed by Goricheva, Krivulin, Evgenii Pazukhin, Natal'ia Malakhovskaia (Goricheva's colleague in the Mariia group), and nine other participants in the seminar. The printed text cites Poresh's multifaceted roles as advocate, organizer, thinker, and educator and highlights the enormous potential of Christianity to enact change in Russian society if believers are willing to do their part: "The harvest is ripe, but the workers are few." It concludes with a broad appeal to "Christians of the whole world and people of good will to prevent reprisal against Vladimir Poresh."

In November 1979, the KGB visited Goricheva's apartment in search of evidence against Poresh. Goricheva refused to provide any potentially incriminating material. Poresh's trial and sentencing took place in April 1980, and Goricheva was exiled from the Soviet Union two months later. Despite the efforts Goricheva and her colleagues made on Poresh's behalf, he received a sentence of five years in the camps and an additional three years of exile within the Soviet Union.

13

Memories of a Keston Information Officer

ALYONA KOJEVNIKOV

How often do we make decisions that change the entire course of our lives, give them a totally new direction? Little did I think when I came to organize the Information Department of Keston College in 1978, that I, hitherto a journalist in the Russian Service of Radio Liberty in Munich, would be involved in so many unexpected and fulfilling activities in the course of my work or that my twelve years as Information Officer of the College would be the most challenging and rewarding period of my life.

The increasing flood of samizdat from the USSR and other communist bloc countries, combined with the rising tide of human rights activities, finally forced the West to acknowledge that the plight of religious believers and human rights activists was an ongoing phenomenon that had to be addressed. By the time I joined the College, Michael Bourdeaux's voice was no longer a lone cry in the wilderness. Assisted by a team of dedicated researchers, Michael's promise to Russian Christians that he would be their voice was being fulfilled. The expertise of Michael's team made the fortnightly Keston News Service bulletin, which was my responsibility, a frequently cited source of information to the media both in the United Kingdom and abroad. We cast our nets wide.

Perhaps the most fulfilling part of my job was maintaining telephone contacts with religious activists in the USSR. Keston's reputation reached them, and they trusted us with the latest information concerning arrests and trials of religious activists. After perestroika, telephone contact with them became easier,

and subsequently many of them are my personal friends to this day. Many knew my voice because Keston loaned me once a week to coauthor and present the religious program of the BBC Russian Service, so that already established my bona fides. I am bilingual, and this made it easier for them to talk with me on the assumption that due to my Russian origins, I would "understand" things that a foreigner might miss. With the growth of Keston's influence, our staff were frequently invited to comment on religious and social events in the USSR on radio and television. This brought me into contact with some of the "movers and shakers" of the time such as the then Prime Minister Margaret Thatcher, for whom I acted as interpreter on numerous occasions, and many others whom I would never have met had I not come to Keston.

We worked hard, and our work was appreciated. We had mana! It was accepted in media circles that "if it comes from Keston College, it can be used without further checking"—a true accolade from the hard-bitten journalists of Reuters, United Press International, Associated Press and so on. I think one of the secrets of our success was that we did not play favorites: we covered the situation of all believers in communist countries with equal care. We were not a campaigning organization, but our material was welcomed by campaigning bodies and individuals. The other secret was teamwork. We were a very mixed bunch, from different countries and from different religious traditions, but we were united in our concern for those who, unlike us, faced daily threat of imprisonment and other persecution for their faith. *E pluribus unum* indeed: "out of many—one." That was us.

14

Unofficial Art from the Soviet Union

LARISA SEAGO

When in 2007 I received an invitation to join the Keston Center for Religion, Politics, and Society at Baylor to care for the Keston Archive that was being shipped to Waco from Oxford, I had no idea how extensive and comprehensive the collection was. The archive arrived in large shipping boxes. The boxes contained records, manuscripts, press clippings, correspondence, publications, audio and video recordings, film reels, photographs, negatives, microfilms, and published and unpublished art. Preserving, organizing, and cataloging such a variety of media is always a challenge. It often involves additional research.

There is a story behind every item in the collection. For me, among the most fascinating items are paintings by Mark Tumin (1946–2013), a nonconformist artist, teacher, and member of the Hermitage group from St. Petersburg. Born in Leningrad, Tumin began learning painting in a studio at the Tavricheskaya Art School. In 1964, he enrolled at the Leningrad Art School. Tumin's teacher, Aleksandr Zaitsev, attended Grigory Dlugach's classes at the Hermitage Museum, to which he invited his students. Meetings with Dlugach changed Tumin's artistic perspective.

An artist, educator, and philosopher, Dlugach gathered a group of young nonconformist artists who shared his dissatisfaction with the "official art" dictated by Soviet ideology. In the 1950s, Dlugach began copying the works of Old Masters in the Hermitage Museum. He developed his own theory of analytical interpretation of a painting based on its "hidden geometry." Unlike traditional academic copying, which focuses on a complete form of a painting, Dlugach's copying focused on the structural principle of its composition. His creativity encouraged his students to discover their own unique styles of artistic expression. Tumin joined Dlugach's Hermitage classes in 1969, and with seven other young artists, created an unofficial collective, the Hermitage Artistic Association.

The most notable series of Tumin's artwork offers gospel themes, portraits, psychological compositions, and analytical interpretations. The Keston Center houses thirteen of his paintings, all untitled and undated. In many of them, Tumin masterfully merges graphic art and painting, using mixed media to add volume. One of the most striking of Tumin's works is the portrait of an old man featured here. The painting is a monotype done with pastel and acrylics. To me, the mostly black-and-white image resembles an icon of St. Nicholas the Wonderworker.

Before 1985, members of the Hermitage Group could not officially exhibit their artwork. Their first unofficial exhibit took place in a private flat in 1974. The situation changed with the beginning of perestroika. Tumin participated in all Hermitage Group exhibits in the former Soviet Union and abroad, held regularly between 1988 and 1997, when the group disbanded.

Before his death in 2013, Tumin achieved international renown. He taught in schools, universities, and studios in the United States and United Kingdom, and helped found a school of composition and develop course curricula for art schools in St. Petersburg, Russia. The Metaphor Artistic Association, founded by Tumin, unites Tumin's former students, who continue the traditions of Dlugach's Hermitage school. The Hermitage Museum, art galleries, and private collections in Russia, western Europe, and the United States house Tumin's work.

Keston received thirteen of Mark Tumin's original paintings from a supporter from East Hampshire. A fellow artist himself, he organized several exhibitions for Tumin in the United Kingdom and donated the paintings to Keston on the artist's behalf in the late 1980s.

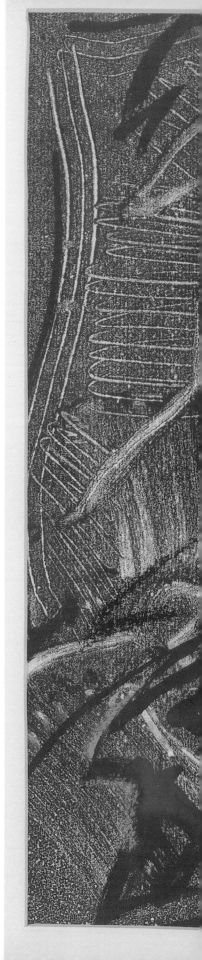

15

A Priest in Exile

MICHAEL BOURDEAUX

The Unknown Homeland is a book-length typescript running to 197 pages. Written anonymously in about 1932, it circulated in a few copies in Russia before one eventually reached the hands of Sir John Lawrence, who donated it to the archive. Two features raise it to the highest level. There are sparkling descriptions of the "homeland." Siberia, the feared place of exile, is iridescent. Then the work answers the question—how did the faith persist during the darkest days of Stalin's persecution?

This was a secret inspiration for years for the small number of believers able to read a copy. The opening is familiar enough: the trudge of a priest, Fr. Pavel, on the *étape* to exile, but the weary prisoner finds inspiration in the beauty of his new surroundings.

The narrative reverts to pre-1917 St. Petersburg, where this scholarly priest gives up a monastic calling to marry a much younger girl and becomes a parish priest instead. His church was soon destroyed by the Bolshevik Revolution. His wife abandoned her faith, but she filed for divorce in an unsuccessful attempt to save him from the raging antireligious persecution.

Testimony to the power of the faith grows as the text progresses. On the exhausting journey Fr. Pavel acquires a disciple, Fyodor, a petty criminal, who makes his confession to the priest. After parish ministry, his "second calling" was to exercise his ministry from his sickbed in an almost inaccessible village.

The heart of the book comes toward the end. As Fr. Pavel's health deteriorated, the bedroom of the peasant's house where he lived in exile became the spiri-

tual center of the village. "Torrents of visitors" arrived, often bringing gifts, as the priest offered the sacraments from his bed.

The prose gains momentum as Fr. Pavel's illness progresses and death approaches. At the end "half the collective farm came to the Zakharovs' house. The priest had lived there for about four months, but for many people he had become their 'adviser', 'benefactor' and 'dear father.'"

On his death, someone remembered that the bell had been saved when the village church had been destroyed, and it was preserved in a cellar. They hauled it out, with great effort erected it on a temporary frame, and rang it over the body of the priest.

Fyodor "was the last to tear himself away from the grave. In the last two days he had wept all his tears and was now overcome by a feeling of supernatural peace. . . . So the story of the exiled pastor came to an end. But though the storm blows over the new and old gravemounds, covering them with snow . . . though time goes by and the years disappear, though no-one comes there any more and the small cross with its worn inscription falls off its base and collapses on to the ground, still the bird-cherry tree will go on arraying itself anew in its wedding colours every spring, and the path of remembrance, prayer and veneration, which leads to such graves, will never be overgrown."

It was over forty years before *The Unknown Homeland* saw the full light of day when Marite Sapiets translated it for Keston and English publication. Eventually, more than sixty years after Fr. Pavel's death, Russian research, guided by a clue in the text about his published study of St. Symeon the New Theologian, revealed his full name: Fr. Pavel Anikiev. This, at last, was followed by publication of the original text in Russia.

Readers of the clandestine text in the 1930s must have found inspiration in this testimony to the Christian faith. How did a Church, beaten to its knees by persecution, not only preserve its faith but pass it on to succeeding generations? *The Unknown Homeland* unlocks the secret.

16

The Lithuanian Memorandum

XENIA DENNEN

The *Memorandum of the Lithuanian Catholic Church* is dated December 1971, and is addressed to Leonid Brezhnev, General Secretary of the Communist Party of the Soviet Union (CPSU). It is a one-page samizdat document, many copies of which were circulated widely in what was then the Lithuanian Soviet Socialist Republic, a part of the USSR, that gathered 17,059 signatures. To sign such a document was a dangerous act and could result in arrest and imprisonment. The document demanded justice, respect for human rights, and religious freedom for a country that was largely Catholic: "We, the Catholics of Lithuania, are deeply disturbed by the violation of these rights, since the believers of our nation are still deprived of freedom of conscience, and the Church is subject to persecution."

A deep ferment against Soviet oppression had been gathering momentum in Lithuania for several years with popular demonstrations and growing discontent. In 1972, the first two issues of the *Chronicle of the Lithuanian Catholic Church*, which contained detailed information about Catholics in Lithuania, reached the West and were translated and publicized by Keston. That year the *Memorandum* was taken by the Catholic activist Nijolė Sadūnaitė to Moscow with the intention of delivering it to Brezhnev, but according to Michael Bourdeaux, she by chance found a British diplomat and gave it to him instead. Thus, the document reached Keston via the diplomatic bag.

In 2005, an exhibition of items from the Keston Archive was organized by the Mažvydas National Library in Vilnius with the *Memorandum* included as the central exhibit. A year later, the Honorary Consul of Lithuania in Wales,

TARYBŲ SĄJUNGOS KOMPARTIJOS GENERALINIAM SEKRETORIUI

MASKVA - KREMLIUS

Lietuvos Rymo katalikų

MEMORANDUMAS

Daug metų pra-ėjo nuo siaubingo karo pabaigos. Tautos pakilo iš griuvėsių ir nori pastovios taikos. Tikros taikos pagrindas yra teisingumas ir žmonių teisių gerbimas. Mes Lietuvos katalikai skaud žiai apgailestaujame, kad iki šios dienos mūsų tautoje yra varžoma tikinčiųjų sąžinės laisvė ir persekiojama Bažnyčia.

Vyskupai Stepobavičius ir Sladkevičius daugiau kaip dešimt metų be teismo sprendimo, be termino yra varginami tremtyje, nors niekuo nėra nusikaltę.

Š.m. lapkričio mėnesį buvo nuteisti metams kalėti du kunigai: J.Zdevskis ir P. Bubnys už tai, kad jie tėvų prašomi bei atlikdami savo kunigiškas pareigas, vaikams paaiškino katalikų tikėjimo pagrindus. Šitie kunigai padėjo vaikams ruoštis pirmajai šv. Komunijai, ne mokykloje, bet bažnyčioje ir niekam prievartos nenaudojo - mokėsi, kas norėjo. Tuo tarpu mokykloje tikinčiųjų tėvų tikintys vaikai prievarta yra mokomi ateizmo, net verčiami kalbėti, rašyti ir elgtis prieš sąžinę, tačiau šitų prievartautojų niekas nebara ir neteisia.

Kunigai nepajėgia mus tikinčiuosius tinkamai aptarnauti, nes jų per maža. Jau daug kur vienas kunigas aptarnauja po dvi, o kartais net tris parapijas. Priversti dirbti net seneliai ir invalidai kunigai. Šitaip yra dėl to, kad Kunigų seminarijos reikalus tvarko ne tiek vyskupas, kiek valdžios įgaliotinis. Valdžia leidžia kasmet į seminariją priimti vos dešimt klierikų. Kunigų skirstymą į parapijas taip pat diriguoja valdžios pareigūnai.

Nors LTSR Baudžiamasis Kodeksas pramato bausmes už tikinčiųjų persekiojimą, bet praktikoje jis niekam netaikomas. 1970 m. Vilkaviškio švietimo skyrius atleido už tikėjimą iš darbo mokyt. Oną Brilienę, o rajono valdžia savame mieste neduoda net šlavėjos darbo. Šitokių pareigūnų niekas nebaudžia, nors dėl jų savavalios inteligentai bijo viešai praktikuoti tikėjimą.

Valdžios pareigūnai neleidžia tikintiesiems savo lėšomis atstatyti sudegusias bažnyčias pav. Sangrūd oje, Batakiuose, Gaurėje. Per didelį vargą leidžiama įsirengti tik koplyčia gyvenamame name, tik jokiu būdu neleidžiama ją persikelti ant šventoriaus.

Mes galėtume nurodyti dar daug persekiojimo atvejų, kurie apkartina mūsų gyvenimą ir sukelia nusivylimą tarybine Konstitucija bei įstatymais. Todėl mes prašome tarybinę vyriausybę suteikti mums sąžinės laisvę, kuri yra užgarantuota TSRS Konstitucijoje, bet iki šiol nebuvo vykdoma. Mes norime ne gražių žodžių per spaudą ir radiją, bet rimtų vyriausybės pastangų, kurios padėtų mums katalikams jaustis lygiateisiais Tarybų Sąjungos piliečiais.

1971m. gruod-žio mėn.

Vyšn

Vyšn

Vyšn

Vyšn

Vyšniausk

Leonov

Paleičienė

Banionienė,

Banionytė,

Banionytė,

Bartkevičienė

Zabitaitė

Zabitaitė

Sukadelskas

Kazakevičus

Kazakevičienė

Kazakevičus

Knutelienė

Račkus

Račkauskienė

Kazakevičienė

Atnanavičienė

Kazakevičius

Kronkevičienė

Kazulevičius

Kazulevičius

Sukadelskienė

Rankienė

Kadel

Vyšn

Sukadelskaitė

Sukadelskaitė

Sukadelskas

Piličiauskaitė

Piličiauskaitė

Piličiauskienė

Balynienė

Balynas

Balynaitė

Balynaitė

Balynas

Maslaveckas

Maslaveckaitė

Mas

Kospul

Stanas

Valanienė

Katalynienė

Katalynaitė

Visockas

Maslaveckienė

Zverszkus

Žvaliauskas

Žvaliauskaitė

Heisav

Mitulevičiūtė

Mitulevičienė

Mitulevičiūtė

Zubauskienė

Kovalauskas

Karoliauskas

Attutienė

Maslava

Kronkevičius

Kronkevičienė

Ruskus

Putkauskaitė

Skiptariauskienė

Kravčinskas

Vyšniauskas

Venckauskienė

Paugonis

Stepanavičius

Paugonienė

Arbo

Lovec

Naveček

Urbonis

Budutov

Žukauskas

Žukauskas

Žukauskienė

Žukauskas

Anthony Packer, wrote to Bourdeaux describing the *Memorandum* as "a treasure of enormous national significance which embodies the spirit of the people in tangible form" and requesting that the document be returned to Lithuania, "in particular to the Lithuanian Church, the fellowship which nourished and sustained the hope which led to its preparation and promulgation during one of the darkest times." With the agreement of Keston members at a general meeting in March 2007, the decision to return the document was taken. In exchange, the Mažvydas National Library agreed to make a facsimile that is now part of the Keston Archive.

In early July 2007, Michael Bourdeaux travelled to Kaunas with the *Memorandum* safely packed into his hand luggage. He was met at the airport by Archbishop Sigitas Tamkevičius, who as a young priest had written the document and organized its circulation as well as editing the *Chronicle of the Lithuanian Catholic Church*. About three quarters of all the copies of the *Memorandum* had been seized by the KGB, but astonishingly, over a hundred survived with over 17,000 signatures. According to Bourdeaux, "The copies were bundled together, and a volunteer found to take them to Moscow . . . The sheets were mostly in poor condition when we received them. After all, they had passed from hand to hand, in and out of deep pockets, while the collection of support went on. But the signatures are as fresh as the day they were written. In blue, black, red or the occasional green they show the hand of the school-teacher as well as of the artisan."

17

Information Flow at Keston

MARK HURST

Accurate and reliable information about believers behind the Iron Curtain was essential to the work of Keston College. Keston drew on an array of material to piece together a picture of what religious life was like in the Soviet bloc. State-approved documents like newspaper articles, academic and literary journals, and other official material were readily accessible, produced by communist authorities in an attempt to control international perspectives on religion under communist rule. These accounts were balanced by samizdat material circulated by individuals and groups that sought to disseminate information independent of the party line. Although samizdat was unpolished in nature, due to its hurried production on cheap, thin paper and its widespread redistribution from person to person, it was invaluable for uncovering the realities of life. The freedom from censorship allowed individuals to discuss their own "truth," something that was particularly valuable when *samizdat* was smuggled to the West and reached those concerned about the treatment of religious believers throughout the Soviet bloc.

The breadth of information collected by Keston College at the height of the Cold War can be clearly seen in this document, which outlines the structure of its Research Department in 1977. This was an important year in the history of human rights. Amnesty International designated it the "Year of the Prisoner of Conscience." Material from a range of sources, including official publications, press from both sides of the Iron Curtain, and information from other activist organizations, was collected, collated, and summarized by Keston researchers. Given the importance of samizdat, it is perhaps of little surprise that "Mike"

RESEARCH DEPARTMENT STRUCTURE

incoming information	reading & summarising		outgoing information	targets

JANE
co-ordination &
control of output

incoming information	reading & summarising		outgoing information	targets
Eastern European books & journals	New researcher(s)		News Service	
Eastern European press	Jane	INFORMATION OFFICER	Telex	PRESS
				MISSIONS
Official Eastern European church publications	Moira		Document Service	RADIO STATIONS
	Marite		Translation Service	CHURCHES & COUNCILS OF CHURCHES
samizdat	Mike		Background Papers	HUMAN RIGHTS ORGANISATION
Western church press	Milena		Case-sheets	
	Veneta	VENETIA typing summaries and recording information	USE OF INFORMATION FILE	
	Alan			
Western secular press				
	Shura			
Western journals & magazines	Chitra		Radio Liberty	THE EAST
press services	Katharine		The Right to Believe	GENERAL PUBLIC
information from missions & other organisations	Kathy	MOIRA controlling flow of documentation	Religion in Communist Lands	SUPPORTERS
	Ella			
			Files	ACADEMICS
	Bärbel			

Bourdeaux, whose call to "be the voice" of the persecuted believer drove Keston, was given the task of processing this valuable material.

Not only does this document highlight which Keston personnel had responsibility for "reading and summarizing" the "incoming information," it also neatly shows how material on religion in the Soviet bloc flowed out of Keston to other interested parties. Keston's researchers funneled information to their "targets" in the wider world, ranging from the press and religious groups to academics and human rights organizations. Jane Ellis, a senior researcher and editor of Keston's academic journal *Religion in Communist Lands*, was responsible for coordinating its output, highlighting her important role in the organization in 1977.

Documents such as this are a rare find for a historian working on activist organizations. Given the pressures on resources and the urgency behind campaigning efforts, groups like Keston rarely reflected on the work they were doing in this manner. This chart offers an invaluable insight into how Keston operated in 1977, capturing how central information, both samizdat and official, was to its work.

18

Sectarians in Soviet Propaganda Posters

ZOE KNOX

Both of these Soviet propaganda posters take aim at Jehovah's Witnesses. The first shows God perched on a cloud, distracted from listening to the radio by four Witnesses. They show him a scroll titled "End of the World" with a series of years crossed off and the word "postponed" scrawled underneath. Another year must be added to the list, and the downcast Witnesses appeal to God, "Would you, creator, clarify when the end of the world is?" The second poster depicts an unkempt man holding *Watchtower* magazine in one hand and swinging an atom bomb from the other. He shouts, "Anti-sovietism . . . anti-communism . . . lies; slander." He stands on a watchtower that serves as a top hat for a crudely drawn face in profile. It has a hook nose and a dollar sign on the cheek and coins for eyes and is set against a backdrop of skyscrapers. The poem reads, "Having covered the Soviet Union with slander / He's forecasting a world war. . . . / Watch out for this persistent sect: / It's dangerous to play war games with them!"

Jehovah's Witnesses were a particular target in an anti-sectarian campaign introduced by Nikita Khrushchev, Stalin's successor, in the late 1950s. The community posed a challenge to communist authorities, who sought to eliminate all forms of social organization beyond the state's control. Witnesses maintained an expansive underground network of believers and even managed to smuggle literature into the USSR from their international headquarters in Brooklyn, New York, reproduce it on hidden printing presses, and distribute it illegally within the community and beyond. Witness congregations met clandestinely to undertake the rites and rituals of their faith, such as baptisms, and to engage in Bible study. Their distinctive lifestyle and practices came to the attention of

the state because they would not fulfill many of the patriotic duties expected of Soviet citizens, such as voting in elections, performing military service, and enrolling children in communist youth groups. Above all else, their continued preaching in the face of sustained persecution frustrated the authorities.

Some of the themes in the posters are common to Soviet anti-Christian propaganda, such as ridiculing the belief that God is powerful and all-knowing. By listening to the radio, presumably to news of the world, God is shown as having no special insight into or influence over worldly affairs. The posters also reveal some Witness beliefs and practices that troubled antireligious propagandists the most. First, they were concerned by Witnesses' success in spreading their apocalyptic message across the USSR despite efforts to eliminate the community that began in the late 1940s. Second, Soviet Witnesses looked to the Brooklyn headquarters for leadership. These links with the United States, which the

authorities could not sever, led propagandists to cast Witnesses as American agents. The backdrop to the second poster was likely intended to be Manhattan, the perceived heart of capitalism. Third, the Kremlin taught that the USSR was peace-loving and the United States was warmongering. The Witness preoccupation with Armageddon was placed within a broader narrative that held that the United States was intent on intensifying the superpower conflict until it climaxed in nuclear war. Finally, by incorporating elements found in anti-Semitic caricatures of Jews, propagandists no doubt meant to insinuate that Soviet Witnesses were loyal to the dollar and not to the USSR.

The posters were produced in 1977 and 1981, respectively. Together they illustrate some of the major tropes used in Soviet anti-Witness propaganda of the period. As such, they tell us much more about the preoccupations of the Soviet state in the final decade of the USSR than they do the religious community they were designed to ridicule and marginalize.

19

Keston Reports Harassment of Uniates

CHRISTOPHER CAMPBELL

At first glance, this Keston News Service (KNS) item appears unremarkable; indeed, it was one of many reports on Soviet religious persecution published by Keston College. It details localized harassment of believers in a remote corner of the Soviet Union, in a small village nestled in the far west of Ukraine, something that was commonplace. Yet, the very existence of a detailed and regular report on religious repression, which relied on sources and testimony from within the Soviet bloc, was truly remarkable. Keston was one of the few western human rights organizations able to maintain clandestine dialogue with religious dissidents in eastern Europe, and KNS was an important platform for publicizing their plight. This particular item is striking both because it highlights several issues affecting Ukrainian Catholic believers in the late 1980s and because it reveals a great deal about the standing of Keston in the region in the final years of the Cold War.

Keston News Service was launched in May 1974, not long after Keston College moved into the premises that would serve as its headquarters until 1991. Up until this point, the organization produced sporadic and informal press releases. KNS was intended to provide a more formal and regular outlet to disseminate details of religious persecution to a wider audience. In the United Kingdom, this included ordinary citizens concerned about conditions for believers in the communist bloc and members of the political elite who, in the mid-to-late 1980s, were increasingly in contact with their Soviet counterparts. Declassified documents in the National Archives in London reveal that KNS reached the highest levels of the British government: Foreign Office officials received a regular copy and took a keen interest in Keston's work.

The Ukrainian Greek Catholic Church, also known as the Uniate Church, benefited from regular coverage in KNS. The Church had been forcibly liquidated and absorbed into the Russian Orthodox Church by Stalinist authorities in 1946. In the early 1980s, Ukrainian Catholics began to emerge from the catacombs and organize into pressure groups calling for the full legalization of the Church and an end to persecution. However, the communist authorities in Kiev remained hard-line, and Uniates continued to suffer. This KNS report reveals that Ukrainian Catholics were enduring harassment even as the Soviet Union entered its final years. The item's mention of the Russian Orthodox Church's complicity is noteworthy.

According to KNS, the security services and the Orthodox Church appear to have been working in concert in the Ukrainian Catholic heartlands, just as in Stalinist times. Perhaps most striking is the information contained in the final paragraph, which states that a letter of protest about the harassment of Uniates had been sent to four high-level individuals. One of these was Keston founder Michael Bourdeaux, named alongside none other than Soviet leader Mikhail Gorbachev!

This item offers a fascinating insight into religious life in Soviet Ukraine and into developments surrounding the Ukrainian Catholic Church and Soviet religious policy in the late 1980s. It is a typical example of the detailed accounts produced by Keston on religious believers under communist regimes at a time when the authorities denied any such persecution was taking place. The regular publication of KNS shone a spotlight on the plight of believers across the Soviet bloc, served as a voice for the voiceless, and stood as witness to the commitment of Keston personnel to the cause of religious freedom.

NEWSDESK

KNS No. 306
4 August 1988
Page 5

AUTHORITIES TRY TO PREVENT UKRAINIAN CATHOLIC GATHERING

The KGB, officials of Lvov *oblast* Council for Religious Affairs, the Russian Orthodox Church and local government workers joined forces in Hrushiv (Grushevo) on 8-11 July to break up a Millennium celebration by the Ukrainian Catholic Church. On 8 July the Russian Orthodox Church reopened the church in Hrushiv which was closed more than forty years ago (then a Catholic church) and which became famous last year when local people reported seeing apparitions of the Blessed Virgin Mary in its belltower and windows (see KNS Nos. 280 and 285). Orthodox priests began conducting services in the church from 9 July in a clear attempt to prevent Ukrainian Catholics from occupying it for their Millennium celebrations. At the same time police forces were stationed on the roads leading to the village to block pilgrims trying to reach it. Despite these preventative measures, 8,000 Ukrainian Catholics came to Hrushiv on 10 July and tried to gain access to the church. They were met by drunken youths and adults at the church gates, with verbal abuse that soon turned to physical assaults with chains, bottles, stones and wooden staves. IVAN HEL, head of the Committee in Defence of the Ukrainian Catholic Church was assaulted, as was the son of Fr PETRO ZELENIUKH. As a result of these attacks some people turned for home, while the remainder - an estimated 5,000 - gathered at some distance from Hrushiv where they erected an eight metre high wooden cross for their celebration. The service was led by Frs Petro Zeleniukh, MYKHAILO HAVRYLIV and MYKOLA KUZ. The Committee in Defence of the Ukrainian Catholic Church collected 1,000 additional signatures to its petition for the legalisation of the Church.

On 11 July the authorities pulled down the cross and removed it to an undisclosed location. Ivan Hel has sent a letter of protest against this action to Lvov *oblast* first secretary POHREBNYK, United Nations General Secretary PEREZ DE CUELLAR, CPSU General Secretary MIKHAIL GORBACHEV and Keston College Director MICHAEL BOURDEAUX. ∎

SOVIET PAPER TALKS TO BILLY GRAHAM

20

Security Police Surveillance in Budapest

JULIE deGRAFFENRIED

With Hungary's incorporation into the Soviet bloc after World War II, the newly formed communist regime adopted the tactics of the Kremlin in dealing with religion. Open terror against clergy, closure of churches, and confiscation of church property characterized communist Hungary, particularly in the 1940s and 1950s. The State Office for Church Affairs, established in 1951, controlled all churches via legal means, operating more or less in symphony with the secret police, whose methods crossed into the extralegal. By the late 1950s, cooperation largely replaced repression. The State Office promised a measure of freedom and small subsidies to religious groups willing to accept and support the regime. "Freedom" meant the ability to accept aid from abroad, more training for seminarians, and permission to organize annual conferences and camps—all elements conducive to maintaining, if not building, communities of faith. The price, though, was high: submission to state intervention in religious affairs.

Tension over this complicated church-state relationship contributed to a split in the Hungarian Methodist Church, a denomination of around a thousand members and no more than two dozen ministers. An elected superintendent governed the Church according to the Methodist Book of Discipline, despite the disruption of its relationship with the international Methodist Church in the late 1940s. While the State Office dealt directly with the "large churches" such as the Catholic Church, it regulated the "small churches" of Hungary, such as the Methodists, via the Council of Free Churches (CFC). Thus, the relationship between the superintendent of the Methodist Church and the head of the CFC was both significant and fraught.

In 1974, conflict over proper procedure within Church administration, fed by longstanding debate over the line between obedience and capitulation, erupted into open war within the Hungarian Methodist Church. Following a disputed superintendent election, a group of ministers led by the ambitious Tibor Iványi, pastor of the large Methodist congregation in Nyíregyháza, hurled charges of corruption at the head of the CFC and accusations of fraud at the leadership of the Methodist Church. The superintendent reprimanded the Iványi group for failing to accept sanction for this disruptive action, and subsequently, the CFC intervened, charging Iványi and his family with anti-state activity and dismissing the entire group of dissenters from ministry, leaving them unemployed. In the following months, at least eight of the Iványi group were arrested and found guilty of charges such as holding illegal meetings or falsification of documents and received suspended sentences. None, however, spent time in prison nor were they prevented from preaching.

Both sides took their arguments to the international community. One Iványi sympathizer traveled to Budapest and took this striking photograph while visiting the Kispest congregation pastored by Gábor Iványi (Tibor's son) and Ilona Vadászi. Since the church building had been sold by the superintendent several weeks previously, members met outside for worship. The pastors pointed out the man with "car trouble" across the street. Posing as a motorist with a broken-down Trabant, this agent had been photographing the congregants' open-air services. Because of the church-state relationship in Hungary, what should have been a denominational conflict involved not only state agencies but also state security. In addition to conducting frequent surveillance of the dissenters, police evicted some members of the Iványi group from rectories, as the Hungarian Methodist Church maintained only licensed ministers could live in them, and restricted other members' communication and mobility by confiscating Church-provided telephones and license plates.

With both sides convinced they were in the right, no reconciliation occurred. Eventually, the Iványi group formed a second Methodist church in Hungary, the Hungarian Evangelical Fellowship, officially recognized by the state in 1981.

21

Raisa Ivanova, True Orthodox Martyr

TATIANA SPEKTOR

The document I am presenting contains a citation from the *#15 Information Bulletin* of the Working Commission to Investigate the Use of Psychiatry for Political Purposes, a major source of information on psychiatric repression in the Soviet Union in 1977–1981. The commission published twenty-two information bulletins and sent them to Soviet officials and out to the West, where those involved in the defense of human rights used them in their campaigns against political abuse in the USSR.

The bulletin informs us that at the end of 1977, Raisa Ivanova, a True Orthodox Christian, allegedly hanged herself in the Kazan special psychiatric clinic. The bulletin's authors did not question the verdict of suicide, but I did. To me, being a "True Orthodox Christian" and committing "suicide" seemed incompatible, so I began to research Raisa Ivanova's case.

I learned that the case had been widely publicized in the late 1970s by Amnesty International, Keston College, *Die Glaube in der Zweiter Welt, les Catacombes, Possev, les Cahiers du Samizdat, Orthodox Life,* and *La Pensée Russe.* Raisa Ivanova was a member of an underground community of True Orthodox Christians in Vladimir, Russia. The True Orthodox, or Catacomb, Church did not recognize the official Moscow Patriarchate, believing that the Patriarchate collaborated with the communist government.

Raisa traveled to Moscow in 1972 together with other members of the Vladimir community and submitted a letter to Patriarch Pimen, head of the Moscow Patriarchate, in which the True Orthodox called upon him to cease collaboration with the antireligious government. Almost immediately after this action,

бираются выписывать в ближайшее время, во всяком случае до Олимпийских игр 1980 года.

ПОЛОЖЕНИЕ НИКОЛАЯ ПЛАХОТНЮКА[1]

Николай Григорьевич ПЛАХОТНЮК по-прежнему находится в психиатрической больнице в г.Смела /Черкасская обл./ в 5-ом отделении /см. ИБ №№5, 7, 8, 12/. У него очень мало надежд на скорую выписку. В разговоре с родственниками врач ПЛАХОТНЮКА заявил, что спешить некуда до окончания Олимпийских игр /!/. Свидания с Николаем ПЛАХОТНЮКОМ не предоставляют, у родственников проверяют паспорта. Прогулки в больнице проводятся редко, зимой их вообще не было, поэтому ПЛАХОТНЮК находится в плохом физическом состоянии.

СУДЬБА РАИСЫ ИВАНОВОЙ

По имеющимся у Рабочей комиссии сведениям, Раиса ИВАНОВА, о которой сообщалось в Информационном бюллетене №2, в 1977 году находилась в Казанской СПБ, куда была направлена из психиатрической больницы[1a] Мордовских лагерей. В Казанской СПБ она подвергалась усиленному лечению, которое переносила очень тяжело. В конце 1977 года Раиса ИВАНОВА повесилась.

УЗНИКИ ПСИХИАТРИЧЕСКИХ БОЛЬНИЦ

СПИНЕНКО Василий, родился в сентябре 1947 г. в г.Макеевка /адрес: Котельный пер., 4/. Был студентом Донецкого политехнического института, затем перевелся на философский факультет Донецкого университета. С 1968 г. принимал[2] участие в организации, которая носила название "партия интеллектуалов"[3] и ставила своей целью добиться передачи власти "интеллектуалам". Организация эта имела членов в нескольких городах Советского Союза, центр ее был в Свердловске.

В марте 1971 г. Василий СПИНЕНКО был арестован. Были аресто-

---

1. В получ.копии здесь и ниже "Плахатнюк" - ошибка.
2. В получ.копии "принимает".
3. Ср.: "революцион. партия интеллектуалистов Сов. Союза" (Хр.33:38).
1а. Точнее: психоизолятор Центральной б-цы.

the True Orthodox participants were arrested and sent to the Soviet republic of Mordovia, to the political zone of the Barashevo prison camp.

Several political prisoners held at this camp at the time passed on information about the Vladimir women to the West, and a Russian émigré newspaper in Paris, *La Pensée Russe*, published an article that described their dignified behavior. They fulfilled the religious obligations of an Orthodox believer with great devotion amid the oppressive camp conditions. Most importantly, they infuriated the camp authorities by their refusal to work in the camp and were severely punished, being placed on a "reduced dietary regime" in a poorly heated punishment cell.

At some point of her prison term between 1974 and 1977, Ivanova was declared insane by the camp administration. It seems that she was a respected figure of authority in her group, and the administration tried to push her to cooperate in the hope of establishing control over the Vladimir women. When these attempts failed, the administration transferred her to Moscow, to the Serbsky Institute for Forensic Psychiatry. To the amazement of all familiar with this institute, Raisa was sent back with a diagnosis of being "in good mental health." Still, the camp administration tried to find some evidence of her supposed mental illness. When the prisoner Kogan, a KGB provocateur, said that Ivanova wanted to kill herself, the officials sent Raisa first to the camp's psychiatric ward and then on to the Kazan psychiatric clinic. Soon after, it was reported that she had died.

While the *#15 Information Bulletin* informs us that she hanged herself in the Kazan psychiatric clinic, other sources claim that she died on the way to that institution while being transferred from the camp. Still others claim that she died in the camp. As I stated earlier, it is extremely doubtful that a practicing Orthodox Christian would commit suicide. It is much more probable that Raisa was hung by the medical aides of the clinic controlled by the KGB. Patients of the Kazan clinic deemed to be too independent or uncooperative routinely suffered such punishment.

22

Buddhist and Shamanic Structures

ROMAN LUNKIN

Taken during a 2009 fieldwork trip made by the Keston encyclopedia team to Blagoveshchensk, Chita and Ulan-Ude, Siberia, these photographs show two religious structures in the Republic of Buryatia, which nestles up against Lake Baikal in Siberia, Russia. The first photo shows the Ivolginsky Datsan near the capital of that region, Ulan-Ude. A *datsan* is a kind of monastery in the Buddhist tradition: it consists of a set of temples and buildings housing statues of Buddhas and storing ancient manuscripts. Ivolginsky was the first datsan to be opened during the Soviet era in 1945, but Buddhism has been in Buryatia since the seventeenth century.

The second photograph shows the headquarters of the Religious Organization of Tengri Shamans with symbols of sun, moon, and earth on the roof. There are several local traditions of shamanism throughout Siberia reflecting the shamanic culture of the native peoples. All of them believe in natural forces that surround us, the heavenly world and the lower world of evil spirits. The shaman as sacral figure acts as mediator between those worlds. Shamanic communities differ from each other by varying interpretations of the world's cosmogony and traditions of healing.

Buddhism and shamanism are traditional religions in Siberia and the Far East. Both enjoyed a revival in the 1990s. This part of Russia is a shining example of the diversity of religious life in the region. The Orthodox Church, though present, is much weaker than local shamanism, Buddhism, or Evangelical Protestantism that emerged here in the post-Soviet era. This results in sometimes syncretic

practices—for example, a person might pray in the Orthodox church but also give a list of names of sick relatives to the datsan requesting healing prayers.

The seven-volume encyclopedia project, titled *Religious Life in Russia Today: A Systematic Description* (*Sovremennaia religioznaia zhizn' Rossii. Opyt sistematicheskogo opisaniia*), conducted by the Keston Institute team covers all regions of Russia from Kaliningrad and Murmansk in northwestern Russia to the Far East of Russia on the borders with China and Japan. The encyclopedia team started its work in the mid-1990s, while regular fieldwork trips began in 1998 and continue to this day. Together with Russian scholars Roman Lunkin and Sergei Filatov, Michael Bourdeaux and Xenia Dennen took part in the field research to experience and document the "real life" of believers through interviews with Orthodox bishops and priests, Protestant pastors, Catholics, Slavic paganists, shamanists, Buddhists, Muslims, Jews, as well as the "new gods" and prophets that organized their own new religious movements. In the encyclopedia, all the richness of the religious culture in today's Russia is described in the sketches on every Russian region with special attention to religious policy, social initiatives, and the state of the freedom of religion or belief. The joy of a social scientist during these trips is to meet sophisticated and outstanding persons who reveal features of the national culture and regional or religious tradition during in-depth interviews. The encyclopedia *Religious Life in Russia Today* is Keston's way to be the voice of believers in academic work. This ongoing field research shows to readers the value of Russia's religious diversity and the new role of religious institutions in a post-secular world.

23

Forum for Church and Human Rights in East Germany

MICHAEL LONG

In the 1980s, two Evangelical Lutheran congregations in Leipzig began to play an increasingly important role in the freedom movement and the struggle for human rights in the German Democratic Republic (GDR), or East Germany. Beginning in November 1982, *Friedensgebete* or "Prayer for Peace" services were held every Monday in the St. Nicholas Church (*Nikolaikirche*), the largest and oldest church in the city. The prayer services developed into full-fledged Monday demonstrations, culminating in the dismantling of the Berlin Wall, the collapse of the GDR government, and the eventual reunification of the two Germanies in 1990.

Building on the momentum created by the prayer services in St. Nicholas Church, Father Christoph Wonneberger of the St. Luke Church (*Sankt Lukaskirche*) organized the Working Group for Human Rights (*Arbeitsgruppe Menschenrechte* or AGM) in September 1986. The AGM's mission was to gather and publicize information on human rights abuses committed by state authorities. In 1989, the AGM began to work very closely with the Working Group for Justice Leipzig (*Arbeitskreis Gerechtigkeit Leipzig* or AKG), which had been organized by students of the Leipzig Theology Seminary in 1987. The AGM and the AKG established a library for samizdat in St. Luke's Church. In September and October 1989, Father Wonneberger's group, the AGM, published its own samizdat newsletter, *Forum for Church and Human Rights* (*Forum für Kirche und Menschenrechte*).

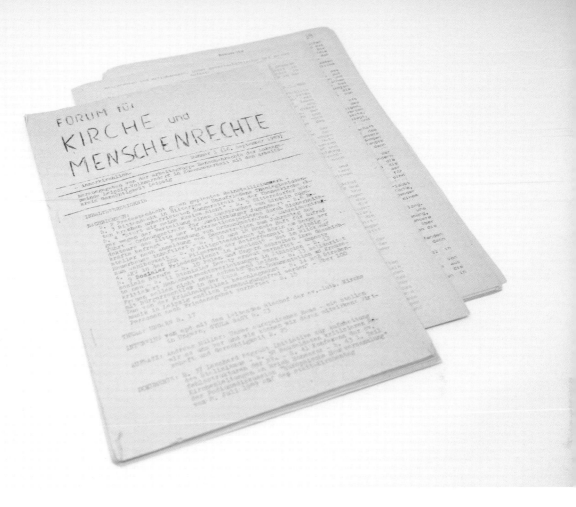

Issue number 1 of *Forum*, dated September 16, 1989, boldly announces, "Published by the Working Group for Human Rights of the St. Luke Church Leipzig-Volkmarsdorf in cooperation with the Working Group for Justice Leipzig." A subheading "for intra-church distribution" completes the masthead. Considering the increasing influence and popularity of the Prayer for Peace services, the *Forum* could have made it into the hands of hundreds, if not thousands, of people. The content of *Forum*, comprising fifty-four typewritten pages of single-spaced text on A4 paper, is comprehensive, rich, and diverse. The AGM did not limit the scope of *Forum* exclusively to issues concerning the GDR but included information and articles on events in Czechoslovakia, Poland, and Hungary as well.

The first fifteen pages of issue 1 are devoted to "News." The news reports cover, among other things: arrests connected with a protest action against a silicon processing plant under construction in Dresden; the end of a hunger strike by theology students in Leipzig; the arrest of two men for hanging posters calling for a boycott of elections in the GDR; protests in Poland, Hungary, and

Czechoslovakia on the anniversary of the August 21, 1968 invasion of Czechoslovakia; and arrests of more than one hundred attendees at the Monday Prayer for Peace services at *Nikolaikirche*. One standout among the news items is a notice to young GDR men who want to avoid the obligatory military service, in which the names and addresses of persons to contact for assistance are also provided. Issue 1 also contains an eight-page report on the situation in Hungary regarding liberalization measures and the role of the Church in the freedom movement. An eleven-page analysis of the socioeconomic condition of the GDR and its place within Europe follows the report on Hungary. Author Andreas Müller asserts, notably, that in comparison with other socialist countries, the GDR is in a much more favorable position economically for integration within Europe due to the country's lack of external debt. Issue 1 concludes with a section of documents, a list of "alternative" community libraries, and a calendar of events related to discussion, information, and seminars concerning the future of the GDR planned through October 31, 1989.

24

Religion, Atheism, and the Family

JULIE deGRAFFENRIED

From 1917, Bolshevik authorities made children a key symbol and indicator of their success in transforming society and creating the "New Soviet Man." They attempted to regulate the environment in which children grew up, both in society and within the home, to instill the values, habits, and upbringing appropriate for the modern, socialist world the Bolsheviks promised to create. This ideal world, of course, did not include religion. The first restriction on the church was aimed at removing its influence over the education of children. Later laws specifically forbade the inclusion of children in faith communities and observances. As alternatives, the state held up its leaders and heroes for children's adulation and provided them secular education and organizations such as the Young Pioneers. To these, authorities added atheist instruction, complete with children's literature, school lessons, field trips, and even toys.

Having done what they could to control religion in the public sphere, state authorities turned to the private sphere: the home. While laws complicated families' efforts to provide children with a religious upbringing, the state found it quite difficult to regulate what happened within the home. Propaganda posters from the late Soviet period, such as the one here by noted graphic artist F. F. Neliubin of the official Militant Pencil (*Boevoi Karandash*) arts collective, reflect this frustration.

Part of a 1979 twenty-three poster collection entitled "We Are Atheists!" (*"My—ateisty!"*), this 28 by 37-centimeter lithograph of Neliubin's original watercolor and gouache work features bright primary colors befitting its young protagonist. A cowlicked boy in the bottom left shows an enormous piece of

— ДЕДУШКА, А Я ЦАРСТВИЕ НЕБЕСНОЕ НАРИ...

Боевой Карандаш

Художник Ф. НЕЛЮБИН
Стихи В. КАПРАЛОВОЙ

Дед видит на примере внука:
Теснит религию наука.

The ol...
of his...
out re...

Th...
ju...

ММ — АГЕНТЫ
«Абонементная подписка «боевого карандаша»
Издательство «издание РСФСР»
№ 667774. Тираж 5000. Заказ 9221. Цена 4 коп.
Ордена Трудового Красного Знамени
типография им. Володарского Ленинград,
191023, Ленинград, Фонтанка 57

86162—162
за7з[85]-79
Издательство «Художник РСФСР», 1979 г.

childish artwork to an old, bearded man on the right. The boy is quite young, as evidenced by his amateurish crayon drawing. The man, bald on top, but with flowing white hair and beard, wears the black gown and pectoral cross of an Orthodox priest. Nose nearly touching the paper, brow furrowed in confusion, he peers closely at the boy's drawing of a satellite, a manned rocket ship, and a smaller spaceship against a blue sky containing golden stars and sun. The child-adult relationship is clarified by the boy's words, depicted in cartoonish, tricolored lettering at the top: "Grandfather, I drew the kingdom of heaven!" A verse at the bottom of the poster provides an interpretation: "The grandfather sees by his grandson's example: / Science pushes out religion."

The victory of science over religion was a common theme in Soviet antireligious propaganda. Here, the boy's depiction of Soviet space technology takes central position within the frame of the poster, emanating golden light. His redefinition of the "kingdom of heaven" uses Christian language but references Khrushchev's famous quote about cosmonaut Yuri Gagarin finding no god in the heavens. Antireligious propaganda posters often depicted children as victims or naïve dupes of religious family members—most often believing grandmothers—but here the child is the teacher. Underscoring the inverted authority, one might read this as a priest's grandson rejecting his family's faith for the state's scientific atheism. The enlightened boy symbolizes the success of the state's entire antireligious campaign: generational, familial, and ecumenical power has been upended.

The very existence of posters like this, however, suggests victory was far from achieved. Having severely delimited the authority of religion via decades of policies and campaigns, the state drove faith into the home. Despite providing Soviet children with atheist education, surrogate holidays and sacred spaces, and new objects of worship, late Soviet antireligious propaganda reflects authorities' lingering anxiety about the family's religious influence on children and the perpetuation of belief.

25

Pilgrimage to Pskov Lavra

STELLA ROCK

The Holy Dormition Pskov Caves Monastery is the only monastic institution in the modern Russian Federation that remained open throughout the Soviet period, partly because it was on the territory of the Estonian Republic until 1940 and incorporated into Soviet Russia with wartime gains. As such, the Caves Monastery, like Pühtitsa Convent in Estonia, was a repository of living religious tradition and an important pilgrimage center for young neophytes as well as those epitomes of Soviet-era Orthodoxy, the white-kerchiefed "grandmothers." In the Moscow Patriarchate, men are expected to remove hats and women to cover their hair in the presence of the divine, and at first glance this photograph seems to reinforce the image of the Russian Orthodox Church as a sea of headscarves. Closer inspection reveals uncovered heads in the foreground, mostly young and middle-aged, at least one of which appears to be female. A significant number of young men in civilian clothes are also clustered around the icon. Their location at the focal point—the sacred center of this public display of piety—may indicate an established relationship with the monastery: these may be resident or repeat pilgrims, or priests' sons helping to manage the crowd.

In this photograph the subjects are unposed and perhaps unaware of or indifferent to the photographer. All their attention is on the flower-bedecked icon visible at the top left-hand corner. A central, ceremonial space demarcated by candle stands and two columns of clergy leads up to the icon. This black and white image cannot reveal the color of the vestments worn by the clergy on the right of the photograph, but they are pale. Many pilgrims hold lit candles, and their dress suggests clement weather. While we cannot see the detail of the icon,

comparison with published photographs indicates that this is the festal icon of the Dormition carried in procession every August 28 (15 Old Style: the feast of the Assumption).

From Khrushchev's antireligious campaign until 1990 this procession was confined within the monastery walls, but as this photograph suggests, such festive celebrations—together with the monastery's famous elders and its sacred topography—continued to attract pilgrims.

How this photograph entered the Keston Archive is unknown. Keston prints of this photograph are undated, but it is also held in the archive of L'Action Chrétienne des Étudiants Russes (ACER), and their copy is labelled 1977. ACER was one of the European organizations with which Keston regularly shared materials, and ACER staff confirm that Jane Ellis, who worked at Keston from 1973, passed on this print. However, since many other ACER photos are marked with the same date in the same hand, 1977 may represent the year that the photo entered the ACER collection rather than the year it was taken. Changes at the monastery in the mid-1970s attracted the attention of human rights activists, but without a certain date or provenance, we have little context for this image.

We have only the immediate archival context, a folder of photographs of pilgrims at the Pskov Lavra, at a holy spring, and at prayer in the forest, which encapsulate the diverse spiritual resources that Soviet believers might draw upon. There are no negatives to confirm whether this selection of prints represents a continuous series of photographs, framing both covert and public but curtailed worship, rebellion and resilience. The prints bear titles in French and/or English (in this case, "Pèlerinage à la Laure de Pskov" in pencil, and "Pilgrimage to Pskov Lavra" in ink, in different hands), plus the stamps of Keston College and ACER. As such, they testify as eloquently to Soviet-era religious activism in western Europe as they do to grassroots religion in late Soviet Russia.

Archival References

All of the material featured in this book is held in the Keston Center for Religion, Politics, and Society at Baylor University, USA.

Cover image

Handwritten transcript from the trial of Aida Skripnikova. Photograph by Carlye Thornton.

Introduction

Keston College. *Georgi Vins and Michael Bourdeaux looking at Vins' autobiography, "Three Generations of Suffering."* 1979. Photograph. Keston Photo Archive (KPA) Box 40/Folder 9.

Keston College. *Malcolm Walker.* N.d. Photograph. KPA Box 90/Folder 8.

Catacombes (October 15, 1971): 1.

"Despre iubire," "Despre muncă," "Despre statornicie." Hand-drawn art. N.d. KA RO/ORT 18/2 LA S.

Nauka i religiia (February 2, 1960): cover.

"Construction Fence . . ." photographs

Keston College. *Warning sign that entrance is forbidden to Chapel of Blessed Xenia because of repairs. Petitions for prayers written on it.* Smolensk Cemetery, Leningrad, July 1986. Photograph. KPA Box 63/Folder 25.

Restoration work continues at the Chapel of the Blessed Xenia. Smolensk Cathedral, Leningrad, August 1985. Photograph. KPA Box 63/Folder 25.

"Czech Dissident . . . Memoir" book

Mlynář, Zdeněk. *Mráz přichází z Kremlu.* Germany: Index, 1981.

"Communist Anti-Islam . . ." poster

Sychёv, Igor Efimovich. Untitled Poster. 1977.

"Siberian Seven" photograph

In front of the Soviet hospital 'Botkin'. January 30, 1982. Photograph. Keston Archive (KA) 76.1/SU/Pen/Siberian Seven/3 of 3.

"The Great . . . Brotherhood" documents

Ermanov letter n.d.; *Velikoe beloe bratsvo* pamphlet n.d.; various press clippings, 1993. KA Jane Ellis Papers/Box 1/Folder 5.

"Sir John Lawrence . . . Advocate" photo

Official Representatives of British Culture, Archangel, 1942. Photograph from unknown source. Keston Photo Archive (KPA) Box 88/Folder 24.

"Father Aleksandr . . . Son of Man" book

Bogoliubov, Andrei. *Syn chelovecheskii.* Brussels: Izdatelstvo "Zhizn' s bogom," 1976.

"Father Aleksandr" photograph

Fr. Aleksandr Men Portrait. N.d. Photograph. KA Su/Ort/Clergy A-Z (2).

"The Trial of Aida Skripnikova" transcript

Hand-scribed linen sheets. 1968. KA SU/Ini 6/7/Aida Trial 1968.

"International . . . Conscience" documents

"Romanian Adventist Could Face Death Sentence." Press Release. October 22, 1984. KA RO/16/4/ Adv 2 Catarama, Dorel (1982–1984).

Handwritten Notes on Dorel Cataramă trial and imprisonment. October 26, 1984. KA RO/16/5/ Adv 2 Catarama, Dorel (1984–1986).

"Council of Prisoners' Relatives" newsletter

Bulletin of the Council of the Relatives of Evangelical Christian-Baptist Prisoners of the USSR No. 27 (1975), KA SU/Ini 11/10 Bulletin S 1975, 28–31.

"The Pope's . . . Poland" photographs

Zywicki, Ɔ. *Pope's Visit to Poland 1979*. Częstochowa, June 6, 1979. Photograph. KPA Box 21/Folder 5.

Rosiński, P. *Meeting with the "KUL" students during Pope's visit to Poland*. Częstochowa, June 6, 1979. Photograph. KPA Box 21/Folder 5.

"Tat'iana Goricheva's . . . Dissident" letter

Goricheva, Tat'iana. Handwritten statement. 1979. KA SU/12/11.1/Christian Seminar.

"Memories of . . . Officer" photograph

Keston College. *Mrs. Alyona Kojevnikov*. 1978. Photograph. KPA Box 90/Folder 8.

Keston College. *Keston publications*. 1984. Photograph. KPA Box 91/Folder 22.

"Unofficial Art . . . Soviet Union" painting

Tumin, Mark. Untitled. N.d.

"A Priest in Exile" *The Unknown Homeland* manuscript

Otchizna Neizvestnaia. Samizdat bound manuscript. KA SU/Ort/S/*Otchizna Neizvestnaya*.

"A Priest in Exile" *The Unknown Homeland* book

The Unknown Homeland. Trans. Marite Sapiets. London: Mowbrays, 1978.

"The Lithuanian Memorandum" artifact

Facsimile of Lithuanian Memorandum, 1971. Gift from National Museum of Lithuania.

"Information Flow at Keston" chart

"Information Flow at Keston." N.d. KA KC Materials/64/2.

"Sectarians . . . Posters" posters

Oboznenko, D. G. (?). *Svideteli iegovy*. Poster. Moskva: Izdatel'stvo "Plakat," 1981.

Efimov, Boris. *Konets sveta*. Poster. 1977 (?).

"Keston Reports . . . Uniates" article

"Authorities Try to Prevent Ukrainian Catholic Gathering." *Keston News Service*, no. 306 (August 4, 1988), 5.

"Security Police . . . Budapest" photograph

Schellenberg, Sandy (?). *Kispest Secret Service, 1977*. Kispest, Hungary. Photograph. KPA Box 14/Folder 13.

"Raisa Ivanova, . . . Martyr" report

Rabochaia komissiia po rassledovaniiu ispol'zovaniia psikhiatrii v politicheskikh tseliakh. *Informatsionnyi biulleten', no 15*. March 8, 1979. KA SU/11/4.21/ Information Bulletin no. 15, 1979.

"Buddhist . . . Structures" photographs

"Keston Encyclopaedia Fieldtrip Russian Far East and Eastern Siberia. Blagoveshchensk, Chita, Ulan-Ude, Moscow (June 12–July 2, 2009)." Report. KA Xenia Dennen Papers/Box 12/Folder 30.

"*Forum . . .* in East Germany" newsletter

Forum fur Kirche und Menschenrechte, 1 (September 16, 1989). Leipzig. KA GDR/18/3.

"Religion, Atheism, and the Family" poster

Neliubin, Fedor. Untitled Poster. In Boevoi karandash, *My—ateisty!* l. 5. Leningrad: Izdatel'stvo "Khudozhnik RSFSR," 1979.

"Pilgrimage to Pskov Lavra" photograph

Pilgramage [sic] *to Pskov Lavra. Soviet Union*. N.d. Photograph. KPA Box 68/Folder 25.

Further Reading

Baran, Emily B. *Dissent on the Margins: How Soviet Jehovah's Witnesses Defied Communism and Lived to Preach About It*. Oxford: Oxford University Press, 2014.

Beliakova, Nadezhda, and Miriam Dobson. "Protestant Women in the Late Soviet Era: Gender, Authority, and Dissent." *Canadian Slavonic Papers* 52, no. 2 (2016): 117–40.

Bociurkiw, Bohdan Rostyslav. *The Ukrainian Greek Catholic Church and the Soviet State, 1939–1950*. Edmonton: Canadian Institute of Ukrainian Studies Press, 1996.

Borenstein, Eliot. "Articles of Faith: The Media Response to Maria Devi Khristos." *Religion* 25, no. 3 (1995): 249–66.

Bourdeaux, Michael. *Land of Crosses: Struggle for Religious Freedom in Lithuania, 1939–78*. London: Augustine Publishing, 1979.

Daniel, Wallace L. *Russia's Uncommon Prophet: Father Aleksandr Men and His Times*. DeKalb: Northern Illinois University Press, 2016.

deGraffenried, Julie. "Combating God and Grandma: The Soviet Antireligious Campaigns and the Battle for Childhood." In *The Dangerous God: Christianity and the Soviet Experiment*, edited by Dominic Erdozain, 32–50. DeKalb: Northern Illinois University Press, 2017.

Ellis, Jane, trans. *An Early Soviet Saint: The Life of Father Zachariah*. London: Mowbrays, 1976.

———. *The Russian Orthodox Church: A Contemporary History*. Bloomington: Indiana University Press, 1986.

Falk, Barbara J. *The Dilemmas of Dissidence in East-Central Europe: Citizen Intellectuals and Philosopher Kings*. Budapest: Central European University Press, 2003.

Fletcher, William G. *The Russian Orthodox Church Underground, 1917–1970*. London: Oxford University Press, 1971.

Goricheva, Tatiana. *Talking about God Is Dangerous: The Diary of a Russian Dissident*. Translated by John Bowden. New York: Crossroad, 1987.

Hurst, Mark. *British Human Rights Organizations and Soviet Dissent, 1965–1985*. London: Bloomsbury, 2016.

Kelly, Catriona. *Socialist Churches: Radical Secularization and the Preservation of the Past in Petrograd and Leningrad, 1918–1988*. DeKalb: Northern Illinois University Press, 2016.

Khalid, Adeeb. *Islam after Communism: Religion and Politics in Central Asia*. Oakland: University of California Press, 2015.

Klein, Olaf Georg. *Suddenly Everything Was Different: German Lives in Upheaval*. Edited by Dwight Allman. Translated by Ann McGlashan. Rochester: Camden House, 2008.

Knox, Zoe. "Preaching the Kingdom Message: The Jehovah's Witnesses and Soviet Secularization." In *State Secularism and Lived Religion in Soviet Russia and Ukraine*, edited by Catherine Wanner, 244–71. Oxford: Oxford University Press, 2012.

———. "Russian Religious Life in the Soviet Era." In *The Oxford Handbook of Russian Religious Thought*, edited by Randall Poole, George Patterson, and Caryl Emerson. Oxford: Oxford University Press, forthcoming.

———. *Russian Society and the Orthodox Church: Religion in Russia after Communism*. London: Routledge, 2005.

Kormina, Jeanne, and Sergey Shtyrkov. "St. Xenia as a Patron Saint of Female Social Suffering: An Essay on Anthropological Hagiology." In *Multiple Moralities and Religions in Post-Soviet Russia*, edited by Jarrett Zigon, 168–90. New York: Berghahn, 2011.

Lawrence, John. *The Hammer and the Cross: Christianity in the Communist World*. London: British Broadcasting Association, 1986.

———. *Russians Observed*. London: Hodder & Stoughton, 1969.

———. *Soviet Russia*. London: Benn, 1967.

Luehrmann, Sonja. *Religion in Secular Archives: Soviet Atheism and Historical Knowledge*. Oxford: Oxford University Press, 2015.

———. *Secularism Soviet Style: Teaching Atheism and Religion in a Volga Republic*. Bloomington: Indiana University Press, 2011.

Mlynář, Zdeněk. *Nightfrost in Prague: The End of Humane Socialism*. Translated by Paul Wilson. New York: Karz Publishers, 1980.

Palmer, Gretta. *Through God's Underground: The Adventures of "Father George" Among People Under Soviet Rule as Told to Gretta Palmer*. London: Hollis & Carter, 1949.

Roberts, Elizabeth, and Ann Shukman, eds. *Christianity for the Twenty-first Century: The Life and Work of Alexander Men.* London: SCM Press, 1996.

Robertson, Jenny. *Be Our Voice: The Story of Michael Bourdeaux and Keston College.* London: Darton, Longman & Todd, 1984.

Rock, Stella. "'They Burned the Pine, but the Place Remains All the Same': Pilgrimage in the Changing Landscape of Soviet Russia." In *State Secularism and Lived Religion in Soviet Russia and Ukraine,* edited by Catherine Wanner, 159–89. Oxford: Oxford University Press, 2012.

Ro'i, Yaacov. *Islam in the Soviet Union: From the Second World War to Gorbachev.* New York: Columbia University Press, 2000.

Steinberg, Mark D., and Catherine Wanner, eds. *Religion, Morality, and Community in Post-Soviet Societies.* Washington, D.C.: Woodrow Wilson Center Press, 2008.

Wanner, Catherine, ed. *State Secularism and Lived Religion in Soviet Russia and Ukraine.* Oxford: Oxford University Press, 2012.

Yusufjonova-Abman, Zamira. "Soviet State Feminism in Muslim Central Asia: Urban and Rural Women in Tajikistan, 1924–1982." PhD diss., University of California Santa Barbara, 2015.

Contributors

Emily B. Baran is Associate Professor of History at Middle Tennessee State University, USA. Her research explores the shifting contours of dissent and religious toleration in the Soviet Empire and its successor states. Her first monograph, *Dissent on the Margins: How Soviet Jehovah's Witnesses Defied Communism and Lived to Preach About It* (Oxford University Press, 2014), charted the history of Jehovah's Witnesses in the Soviet Union and post-Soviet Russia, Ukraine, and Moldova.

Canon Michael Bourdeaux graduated from Oxford University, UK, with degrees in Russian and French and then Theology. After an academic year at Moscow University, USSR, together with colleagues he founded Keston College in 1969, the archive of which moved from Oxford to Baylor University in 2007. In 1984 he was awarded the Templeton Prize for Progress in Religion in recognition of his work.

Christopher Campbell is a PhD student in history at the University of Glasgow, UK. His research interests include the religious and diplomatic history of the Cold War, Soviet church-state relations, the role of religion in foreign policy, and international religious freedom. His thesis explores the religious revival in Soviet Ukraine during the final years of the Cold War and how this was aided by western governments and organizations.

Wallace L. Daniel is Distinguished University Professor of History at Mercer University, USA. His present research interests focus on religion and culture in post-Soviet Russia. His most recent book is *Russia's Uncommon Prophet: Father Aleksandr Men and His Times* (Northern Illinois University Press, 2016).

Julie deGraffenried is Associate Professor of Russian and East European History at Baylor University, USA. Recent publications include *Sacrificing Childhood: Children and the Soviet State in the Great Patriotic War* (University Press of Kansas, 2014) and chapters in *The Dangerous God: Christianity and the Soviet Experiment* (Northern Illinois University Press, 2017) and *War and Childhood in the Era of the Two World Wars* (Cambridge, 2019). Her research interests include children and childhood, war, children's culture, and religion in the Soviet Union.

Xenia Dennen was a founder of Keston College in 1969, a member of the research staff, and the first editor of its academic journal, *Religion in Communist Lands*. She acted as Keston's Moscow representative from 1992 to 1999 and joined the organization's encyclopedia team in 2000. She has been Chairman of Keston Institute UK since 2002.

April L. French is a PhD candidate in history at Brandeis University, USA. Her research interests center around the theology and everyday practice of religious believers in the Soviet Union. She is writing a dissertation on evangelical women in late Soviet Siberia. Her publications include the edited translation of *An Inner Step Toward God: Writings and Teachings on Prayer by Father Alexander Men* (Paraclete Press, 2014) and a recent article in *Gosudarstvo, religiia, tserkov' v Rossii i za rubezhom* (*State, Religion and Church in Russia and Worldwide*) on Michael Bourdeaux and the early years of Keston College.

Kathy R. Hillman is Associate Professor in the Baylor University Libraries where she holds the titles of Director of Baptist Collections and Library Advancement as well as Director of the Keston Center for Religion, Politics, and Society. She has published prolifically in Baptist publications and is a member of the Keston Institute UK Council of Management. She earned a Bachelor of Arts from Baylor in communications and a Master of Library Science from the University of North Texas, USA.

Mark Hurst is Lecturer in the History of Human Rights at Lancaster University, UK. His research focuses on the contemporary history of human rights, political dissent, and activism in the Cold War. His recent publications include *British Human Rights Organizations and Soviet Dissent, 1965–1985* (Bloomsbury, 2017) and "Slowing down the going-away process: Tom Stoppard and Soviet Dissent," *Contemporary British History* 30, no. 4 (2016).

Zoe Knox is Associate Professor of Modern Russian History at the University of Leicester, UK. Her research explores issues of religious tolerance and intolerance in the modern world, in Russia and beyond. Her publications include *Russian Society and the Orthodox Church: Religion in Russia after Communism* (Routledge, 2005) and *Jehovah's Witnesses and the Secular World: From the 1870s to the Present* (Palgrave Macmillan, 2018).

Alyona Kojevnikov read Russian Language and Literature at Melbourne University, Australia. In 1971, she began work at the Russian Service of Radio Liberty in Munich. Later that decade, she became Information Officer for Keston College, having met Michael Bourdeaux at an international conference in 1975. In the early 1990s, Kojevnikov was named the Bureau Chief at Radio Liberty in Moscow and set up the Radio Liberty operation from scratch. She has translated numerous books from Russian into English, including Irina Ratushinskaya's *Grey is the Colour of Hope* (Hodder & Stoughton, 1988) and Vladimir Bukovsky's *Judgement in Moscow* (Ninth of November Press, 2019).

Michael Long is Professor of Russian at Baylor University, USA. His research interests are primarily dissidence in the former East Bloc and Soviet Union and the restoration of cultural monuments in post-Soviet Georgia. Long is the author of *Making History: Czech Voices of Dissent and the Revolution of 1989* (Rowman & Littlefield, 2005), an oral history of the Velvet Revolution, and "Collaboration, Confrontation, and Controversy: the Politics of Monument Restoration in Georgia and the Case of Bagrati Cathedral," *Nationalities Papers* 45, no. 4 (2017).

Sonja Luehrmann is Associate Professor of Anthropology at Simon Fraser University, Canada. Her research focuses on religion, atheism, and the politics of gender and family in Soviet and post-Soviet Russia. Her publications include *Secularism Soviet Style: Teaching Atheism and Religion in a Volga Republic* (Indiana University Press, 2011); *Religion in Secular Archives: Soviet Atheism and Historical Knowledge* (Oxford University Press, 2015); and the edited collection *Praying with the Senses: Contemporary Orthodox Christian Spirituality in Practice* (Indiana University Press, 2018).

Roman Lunkin is Director of the Center for Religious Studies in the Institute of Europe at the Russian Academy of Sciences and is affiliated with the Kennan Institute at the Woodrow Wilson Center in Washington, D.C. Since 1998, he has been a member of the Russian team working on Keston's "Encyclopedia of Religious Life in Russia Today" project. His research focuses on Christianity and democracy, religious institutions in civil society, religious freedom, and interreligious dialogue.

Stella Rock is Associate Lecturer and Honorary Associate in Religious Studies at the Open University, UK, and an honorary Senior Researcher at the Institute for the Study of Eastern Christianity, Vrije Universiteit, the Netherlands. Her broad research area is Russian Orthodox Christianity, with a focus on lived religion and the relationship between religion, historical memory, and identity. Recent publications include chapters in the edited books *International Perspectives on Pilgrimage Studies: Itineraries, Gaps and Obstacles* (Routledge, 2015) and *Framing Mary: The Mother of God in Modern, Revolutionary, and Post-Soviet Russian Culture* (Northern Illinois Press, 2018).

Larisa Seago is a library information specialist in the Keston Center for Religion, Politics, and Society in the Baylor University Libraries. A native of Samara, Russia, she began work at Baylor in 2003. Since 2007, Larisa has been the Curator of the Keston Archive and Library and assists researchers at the Keston Center. In 2013, she completed a master's degree in Church-State Studies at Baylor's J.M. Dawson Institute for Church-State Studies.

Elizabeth Skomp is Professor of Russian and Associate Dean for Faculty Development and Inclusion at Sewanee: The University of the South, USA. Her research focuses primarily on Russian women writers of the twentieth and twenty-first centuries. She is the author (with Benjamin Sutcliffe) of *Ludmila Ulitskaya and the Art of Tolerance* (University of Wisconsin Press, 2015).

Tatiana Spektor (Sister Alexandra) is a member of the monastic community of the Lesna Russian Orthodox Monastery in France. Previously a professor of Russian at Iowa State University, USA, Spektor continues to write and present conference papers on Orthodox Christian themes in Russian literature and Russian Orthodox Church history. Her publications include the edited collection (with Byron Lindsey) *Routes of Passage: Essays on the Fiction of Vladimir Makanin* (Slavica Publishers, 2007) and *Tserkovnoe soprotivlenie v SSSR: 1920-e* (*Religious Resistance in the USSR: 1920s*) (Duh i Litera, 2019).

Alina Urs is an associated researcher in the Center for Studies in Contemporary History, Romania. Her latest book (with Constantin Vasilescu and Lucian Vasile) is *Traversând comunismul. Conviețuire, conformism, compromis* (*Living through Communism: Cohabitation, Conformism, Compromise*) (Polirom, 2016).